W9-AZG-503

TAIGA

Trevor Day

www.heinemannraintree.com
Visit our website to find out
more information about
Heinemann-Raintree books.

To order:
☎ Phone 888-454-2279
💻 Visit www.heinemannraintree.com
to browse our catalog and order online.

Published in 2011 by Heinemann-Raintree books, an imprint of Capstone Global
Library, LLC, Chicago, Illinois

© 2011 The Brown Reference Group Ltd.

For The Brown Reference Group Ltd:
Editorial Director: Lindsey Lowe
Managing Editor: Tim Harris
Editor: Jolyon Goddard
Original consultant: Dr. Mark Hostetler,
Department of Wildlife Ecology and Conservation, University of Florida
Designers: Reg Cox, Joan Curtis
Picture researcher: Clare Newman
Production Director: Alastair Gourlay

Printed in the USA

ISBN: 978-1-432-94179-6; 978-1-432-94184-0 (set)
14 13 12 11 10
10 9 8 7 6 5 4 3 2 1

Library of Congress Cataloging-in-Publication Data

Day, Trevor.
  Taiga / Trevor Day.
      p. cm.—(Biomes atlases)
  Includes bibliographical references and index.
  ISBN 978-1-4329-4179-6 (hc)
1. Taiga ecology—Juvenile literature. 2. Taiga ecology—Maps for children.
I. Title.
  QH541.5.T3D39 2011
  577.3'7—dc22   2010013027

About this Book

This book's introductory pages
describe the biomes of the world and
then the taiga biome. The five main
chapters look at aspects of the taiga:
climate, plants, animals, people, and
the future. Between the chapters are
detailed maps that focus on key taiga
regions. The map pages are shown in
the contents in italics, *like this*.
Exclamation-point icons on the map
pages draw attention to regions where
the biome or its wildlife is under threat.
Throughout the book you'll also find
boxed stories or fact files about the
taiga. The icons here show what the
boxes are about. Words in **bold**
throughout the book are explained
in the glossary at the end of the
book. After that is a list of books
and websites for further research
and an index, allowing you to locate
subjects anywhere in the book.

 Climate

 People

 Plants

 Future

 Animals

 Facts

 Under Threat

Contents

Biomes of the World   4

The Taiga Biome   6

Northwestern American Taiga   8

Taiga Climate   10

Northeastern American Taiga   18

Taiga Plants   20

European Taiga   30

Taiga Animals   32

Siberian Taiga   44

People and the Taiga   46

East Asian Taiga   54

The Future   56

Glossary   62

Further Research   63

Index   64

BIOMES OF THE WORLD

Biologists divide the living world into major zones named biomes. Each biome has its own distinctive climate, plants, and animals.

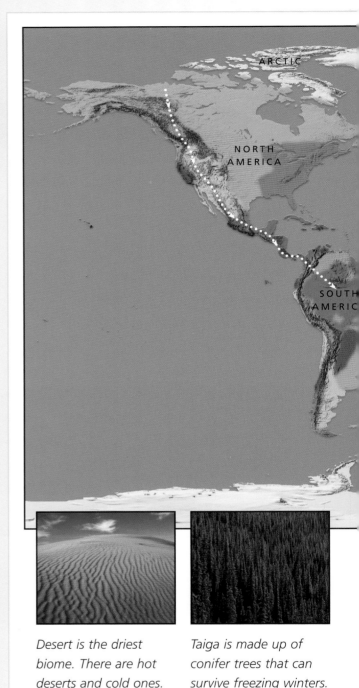

Desert is the driest biome. There are hot deserts and cold ones.

Taiga is made up of conifer trees that can survive freezing winters.

If you were to walk all the way from the north of Canada to the Amazon **rain forest**, you'd notice the wilderness changing dramatically along the way (see route marked on map to right).

Northern Canada is a freezing and barren place without trees, where only tiny brownish-green plants can survive in the icy ground. But trudge south for long enough and you enter a magical world of **conifer** forests, where moose, caribou, and wolves live. After several weeks, the conifers disappear, and you reach the grass-covered prairies of the central United States. The farther south you go, the drier the land gets and the hotter the sunshine feels, until you find yourself hiking through a cactus-filled **desert**. But once you reach southern Mexico, the cacti start to disappear, and strange **tropical** trees begin to take their place. Here, the muggy air is filled with the calls of exotic birds and the drone of tropical insects. Finally, in Colombia you cross the Andes mountain range—whose chilly peaks remind you a little of your starting point—and descend into the dense, swampy jungles of the Amazon rain forest.

Scientists have a special name for the different regions—such as desert, tropical rain forest, and prairie—that you'd pass through on such a journey. They call them **biomes**. Everywhere on Earth can be classified as being in one biome or another, and the same biome often appears in lots of

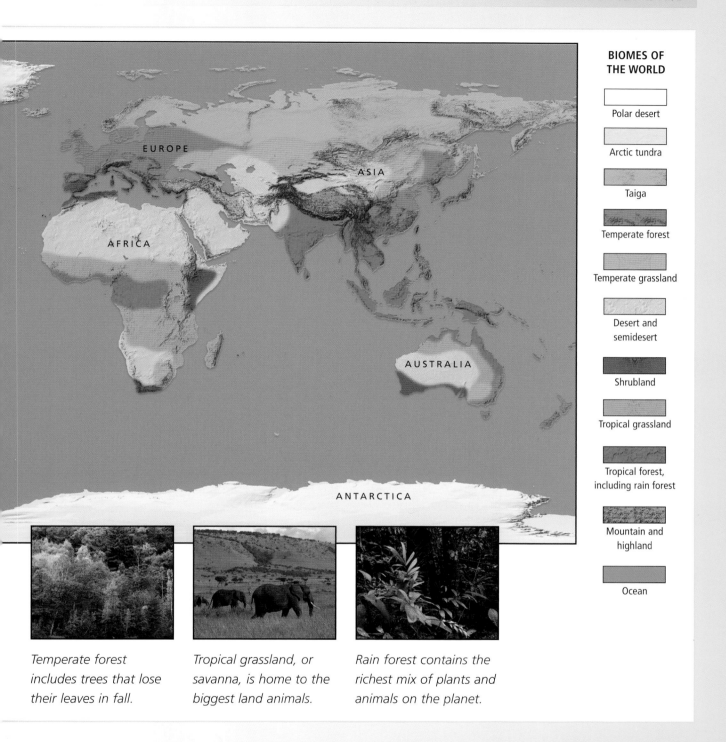

BIOMES OF THE WORLD

Polar desert

Arctic tundra

Taiga

Temperate forest

Temperate grassland

Desert and semidesert

Shrubland

Tropical grassland

Tropical forest, including rain forest

Mountain and highland

Ocean

EUROPE

ASIA

AFRICA

AUSTRALIA

ANTARCTICA

Temperate forest includes trees that lose their leaves in fall.

Tropical grassland, or savanna, is home to the biggest land animals.

Rain forest contains the richest mix of plants and animals on the planet.

different places. For instance, there are areas of rain forest as far apart as Brazil, Africa, and Southeast Asia. Although the plants and animals that inhabit these forests are different, they live in similar ways. Likewise, the prairies of North America are part of the grassland biome, which also occurs in China, Australia, and Argentina. Wherever there are grasslands, there are grazing animals that feed on the grass, as well as large carnivores that hunt and kill the grazers.

The map on this page shows how the world's major biomes fit together to make up the biosphere—the zone of life on Earth.

THE TAIGA BIOME

Taiga forests occupy a larger area than all the tropical rain forests. They grow in a region of extreme weather encircling the northern hemisphere from Alaska to Japan.

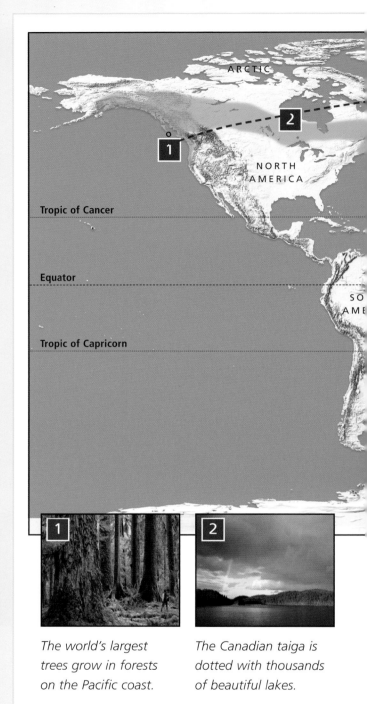

Tropic of Cancer

Equator

Tropic of Capricorn

ARCTIC

NORTH AMERICA

SOUTH AMERICA

The world's largest trees grow in forests on the Pacific coast.

The Canadian taiga is dotted with thousands of beautiful lakes.

Taiga (pronounced tie-guh) occupies about one-tenth of Earth's land surface, and as a land biome it is second in size only to deserts. The forests that grow in the taiga biome are filled with mainly conifer trees. Conifer trees keep their leaves all year round and produce cones rather than flowers. Often, only two or three conifer species, such as spruces, pines, or firs, cover large areas of the forest.

Most of the taiga grows in icy land near the arctic circle—the coldest place in which full-size trees can grow. This sort of taiga is called boreal forest. Some people use the terms *taiga* and *boreal forest* interchangeably. However, taiga forest also grows farther south, such as along the northwest coast of North America. There is so much rainfall there that the taiga is described as rain forest. Despite this name, these forests are filled mainly with conifers and are more similar to boreal forests than to the tropical rain forests around the **equator**.

The word *taiga* comes from the Russian word for "marshy pine forest," which is a very apt description. Boreal forest is named for *Boreas*, the Greek god of the north wind.

Beyond the northern limit of taiga, it's too cold for full-size trees to grow, and **tundra**—a biome with plants no larger than shrubs—replaces taiga. At its southern limit, taiga gives way to forests of broad-leaved trees and **temperate** grasslands. In between, vast areas of the taiga form dense forest. However, the

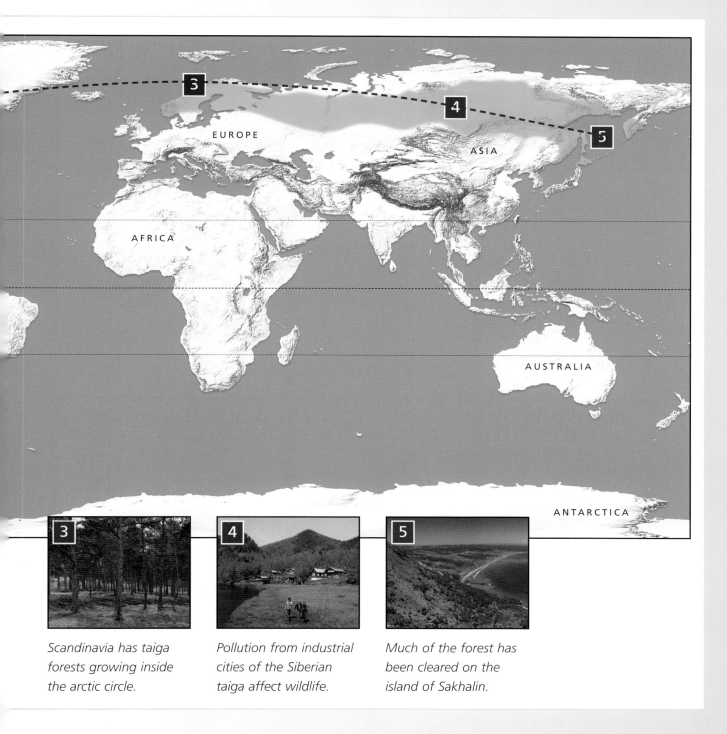

Scandinavia has taiga forests growing inside the arctic circle.

Pollution from industrial cities of the Siberian taiga affect wildlife.

Much of the forest has been cleared on the island of Sakhalin.

landscape sometimes creates a jigsaw puzzle of forests, wetlands, and lakes.

Taiga covers much of Alaska and Canada and extends as far south as northern Upstate New York, Vermont, New Hampshire, and Maine. Scotland has a few patches of taiga. From Scandinavia to the eastern coast of Siberia there is an unbroken swath of taiga. It is also found in northern Japan.

Much of the world's softwood for timber and paper comes from taiga. It also holds reserves of fossil fuels. Due to its enormous size and harsh weather, the taiga is sparsely populated and much of it remains a pristine wilderness.

NORTHWESTERN AMERICAN TAIGA

The western belt of North American taiga is a mosaic of forests, rivers, and lakes. It gives way to barren tundra in the north and vast prairie grasslands to the south.

A hiker surveys the enormous trees and lush vegetation of the Hoh Rain Forest in the mountains of northwest Washington State.

Fact File

▲ Canada has more lakes than any other country. Most of them are in the taiga region.

▲ Many of the plants, especially mosses, in the rain forests of the Pacific Northwest are epiphytes—they grow on the trunks and branches of trees.

▲ The sandy soil south of Lake Athabasca is oozing with tar and oil—the largest deposit of its kind in the world. Oil workers clear the forest and dig up the sand to extract the useful substances. However, this mining disrupts wildlife in the region. In addition, the burning of fossil fuels, such as oil, causes climate change and global warming—the gradual warming of Earth's climate because of pollution in the atmosphere.

Rain Forest

The forest along the Pacific coast from Oregon to Alaska is so wet that it is called a rain forest. With so much rain, this forest is much lusher than the rest of the taiga. In fact, the plants along this coast grow even taller than those in tropical areas. Some trees in the region have been growing for more than 2,000 years.

1. Kodiak Island
Russian settlers arrived in on the island in 1784. Kodiak bears—the largest type of brown bears—are common. Male bears reach up to 680 kilograms (1,500 pounds) in weight.

2. Denali National Park and Mount McKinley
The world's second-largest taiga reserve includes Mount McKinley, the tallest point in North America at 6,194 meters (20,320 feet).

3. Alexander Archipelago
A group of islands that are home to Alaska's Haida people. Deforestation threatens the islands' wildlife.

4. Olympic National Park
Luxuriant mountain rain forest on the coast of Washington. The Elwha River dam (inset) in the park is due to be dismantled. This will revive wetland habitats and allow salmon to swim upstream to breed.

5. Great Bear Rain Forest
The largest of North America's Pacific rain forests. It is home to grizzly and Kermode bears and 1,000-year-old trees.

6. Yukon
A remote area of mountains, forests, and plateaus. In recent years, global warming has caused an abundance of insects that live off and kill trees. In addition, warmer waters are causing diseases of fish.

7. Rocky Mountains
The Rockies run nearly 4,800 kilometers (3,000 miles) from Alaska in the north to Mexico in the south. Global warming is causing rapid melting of the glaciers in the mountains.

8. Mackenzie River and Great Slave Lake
Canada's longest river flows from the Great Slave Lake to the Arctic Ocean. Oil and gas mining threaten wildlife in the river and lake.

TAIGA CLIMATE

For most of the year, taiga is dark, cold, and covered in snow and ice. During the short periods of warmth in spring and summer, the days get longer, the ice and snow melt, and the forest comes to life.

The climate of taiga forest is very harsh, with snow and ice covering the ground for much of the year. The plant life is shrouded in water, but this water is in a frozen form that plants cannot use. During the long winter, plants endure a water shortage as severe as that in deserts. However, with the spring thaw, the reverse is true, and there is an abundance of liquid water. Now, plants have to cope with soils that are very damp or have had all the **nutrients** washed out of them. Despite all these difficulties, conifer trees thrive in taiga forests.

Around the World

As with other land biomes, taiga exists because the particular combination of **climate** and soil favors certain kinds of plants. The long, cool winters and short, warm summers of this biome occur in lowlands in the far

A thick layer of snow weighs down conifer trees in a foggy forest in Norway. Taiga forests are covered in snow for most of the year.

north of North America, Europe, and Asia. Similar conditions also exist farther south on the slopes of tall mountains, and taigalike forests grow there, too. No taiga forest grows in the southern **hemisphere**. This is because the area where taiga would grow is mainly covered by ocean.

Taiga develops where the growing season for plants is at least three months, and where the average daily temperature in the warmest month of the year is about 10°C (50°F). In winter, temperatures in some taiga forests can be even lower than in the Arctic tundra to the north. In fact, northern Siberia is one of the coldest places on Earth—chillier than anywhere, except for Antarctica. In much of Siberia, differences between summer and winter temperatures are also among the largest anywhere. In winter, temperatures can plunge to as low as -68°C (-90°F), while in summer they soar to 30°C (86°F)—a temperature range approaching a phenomenal 100°C (180°F).

The taiga may be cold for much of the year, but the presence of snow can benefit plants. Snow acts like a fluffy, air-filled jacket, insulating trees and soil from the bitterly cold air. In winter, the soil at a depth of 50 centimeters (20 inches) can be 20°C (36°F) warmer than the air above. At these depths, tree roots are still able to take in life-giving water, even though the temperatures above ground are well below freezing.

Hardy Trees

Conifers dominate the taiga. Few broad-leaved, **deciduous** trees, which shed their leaves each year, survive in the biome. Because taiga areas have such short growing seasons, deciduous trees are at a disadvantage.

Right: Needles of a white pine tree dripping with meltwater. When the snow and ice melt, taiga forests become very wet indeed.

Mountainside Forests

Well beyond the southern limit of lowland boreal taiga, conifer forests grow on mountain slopes where temperatures are much cooler than surrounding low-lying areas. The trees in these high-altitude (high above sea level) forests are very similar to those that live in areas of boreal taiga. For example, the highland forests of the Alps and Pyrenees mountains in Europe contain the same species of pine and fir tree that grow in the taiga forests in the far north of Europe.

Earth is warmer near the equator than at the poles. Therefore, as a general rule, the mountains that are farther south, and farther from true taiga forest, have taigalike conditions higher up and are home to more nontaiga trees. Near the northern end of the Rocky Mountains in North America (below), conifer forests grow to a timberline (the upper limit of tree growth) at an altitude of only 1,500 meters (4,900 feet). In the warmer, more southerly Rockies of Colorado, the belt of conifer forest begins at an altitude of about 2,130 meters (6,900 feet) and the timberline reaches to about 3,200 meters (9,900 feet) above sea level.

Plants **photosynthesize** (make food from sunlight) with their leaves. Each spring, deciduous trees must grow a new set of leaves, which they then shed when the weather gets cooler in the fall. This is very wasteful if the growing season is only short. Coniferous evergreens keep their needlelike leaves for several years. They are, therefore, ready to photosynthesize and grow as soon as spring begins.

Humid Summers

The conifer trees of the taiga are well suited to coping with cold and dampness, but they cannot tolerate warmth coupled with dryness. Taiga trees grown outside their biome, such as in arboretums and gardens, do not do as well as those in the taiga. Even with plenty of water in summer, the trees still fare poorly if the air is dry. They lose water through their needles and grow to only a fraction of the size they would reach in the taiga. Spruces cultivated in warm climates grow to half their natural height.

Waterlogged Soil

The layered soil of taiga forest is called podzol, from the Russian word for ash, which describes the color of one of the soil's layers. Podzol forms because taiga climates are so cold, and because the pine needles shed by conifers are broken down very slowly by decomposers in the soil. As a result, the ground becomes covered in a thick layer of pine needles and other debris shed by trees. These layers eventually form podzol.

The combination of cold and wet conditions, plus slowly decaying plant matter, makes the upper region of the soil acidic. Over the course of a year, the amount of water falling as snow, rain, or hail is much greater than that rising into the air by evaporation. The extra water sinks down, mixing with the acidic soil. This acid-rich

In the short summer, taiga forest is bathed in warm sunshine during very long days. At the northern limit of the taiga, the Sun sets for only a few hours a day.

Western Mountain Forests

On North America's Pacific coast, running from Alaska and Canada in the north to California in the south, coniferous forests clothe the western mountain ranges. Here, winters are milder and wetter than in other northern forests, but the plant life is similar to boreal taiga: pine, fir, spruce, hemlock, and larch.

The forests receive an enormous amount of rain—nearly 4.3 meters (14 feet) every year, and they are named rain forests because of this. The coastal mountains trap the wind blowing in from the ocean, and this moist wind releases its rain as it rises up the mountainside. The western slopes get all the rain, while the region to the east of the mountains is much drier.

The mountains also protect the rain forests from the icy air that travels down from the arctic. On the coast, the temperature rarely drops below freezing, while on the eastern side of the mountains, the forests must cope with much colder weather.

Being so wet, the forests have an almost tropical luxuriance, with an undergrowth of ferns, mosses, and lichens. In north California and southwest Oregon, the forests are infiltrated by giant redwoods (above), the largest trees on Earth. The Redwood National Park of northern California is home to the biggest tree in the world—a 112-meter (367-foot) coast redwood. Its bark is nearly 30 centimeters (1 foot) thick.

Climographs

Each place in the world has its own pattern of weather. The typical pattern of weather that happens in one place during a year is called climate. We can sum up a place's climate on a climograph, such as the one shown here for St. Louis. The letters along the bottom are the months of the year. The numbers on the left and the small bars show rainfall, and the numbers on the right and the curvy line show temperature. You can see at a glance that St. Louis is hottest in July, but December is the driest month.

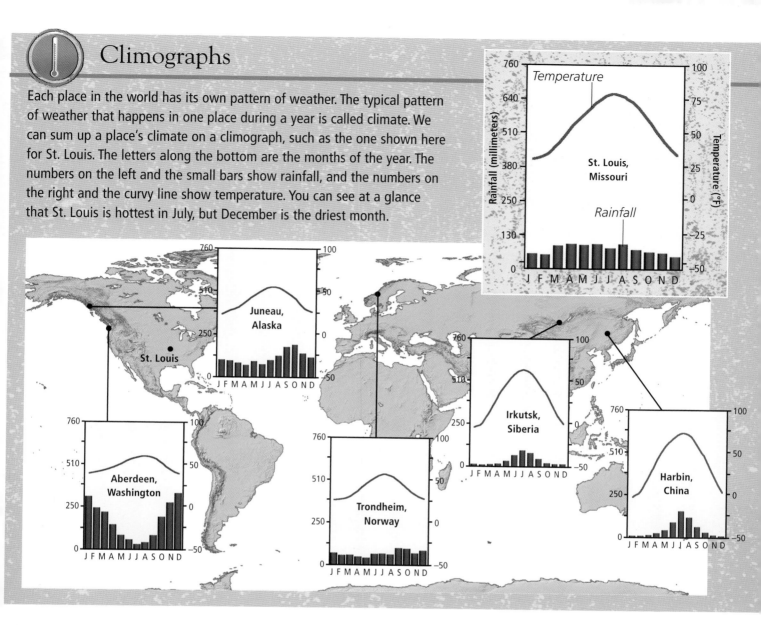

water dissolves metals such as iron and aluminum from the soil and deposits them deeper down. Sometimes, iron-rich layers called iron pans develop. Iron pans stop water from draining deeper into the ground. As a result, the soil above the iron pan becomes completely filled with water and this water drives all the air out of the soil.

In these conditions, plant material decomposes even more slowly. Over many hundreds of years, it accumulates to form **peat**—a brown mass of partially decayed vegetation. Dried peat can be burned as fuel. When peat is burned, the sunlight energy trapped by plants hundreds or thousands of years ago is released as heat.

History from the Soil

Scientists can unlock the ancient history of the taiga from its peat. **Pollen** grains—the microscopic capsules that contain the male sex cells of trees and other plants—are as recognizable as the flowers from which they come. But while flowers are fragile, pollen grains have a protective covering, like armor. They can survive in peat for thousands of years.

The deeper the layer of peat, the older it is. Scientists collect the pollen grains from different layers and identify and count the grains under the microscope. This tells them which trees grew nearby thousands of years ago. It also tells them something about the climate at the time, and how this has changed over the years. Changes in climate produce changes in plant life. The record of buried pollen charts the comings and goings of different plant species through time.

Permafrost

In parts of northern Canada and much of Siberia, the taiga grows above a solid layer of frozen ground. This permanently frosty soil is called **permafrost**. About 1 meter (39 inches) below the surface, the soil is rock-solid ice. Tree roots cannot penetrate this icy barrier and spread sideways to collect water.

The permafrost stops water from draining away, so the soil above becomes saturated with water. The trees themselves help create the

Black spruce trees growing in open taiga in Labrador, Canada. The trees grow thickly in sheltered areas but are more scattered in exposed places.

permafrost because they absorb the Sun's heat, preventing it from reaching the icy ground. In parts of Siberia, the permafrost extends to more than about 1,250 meters (4,000 feet) deep. Seeds buried in permafrost can be held in suspended animation for thousands of years. Most of the preserved seeds die, but just occasionally scientists manage to make one sprout into a plant. Such plants are often different from those found in the taiga today. This shows how climate and plant life in the region have changed over thousands of years.

Open and Closed Taiga

At the northern edge of the taiga, the temperatures are almost too cold for trees to survive. Farther to the north, the trees give way to open tundra, while to the south of this boundary, open taiga grows. Because of

Moss grows in a boggy clearing in a Siberian forest. This area is free of trees because the ground is far too wet for them to grow.

the cold, the trees growing in open taiga are generally small and lean and more widely spaced than the trees growing farther south. In North America, open taiga is dominated by black spruce. Between the widely spaced trees, plenty of sunlight reaches the ground. Lichens, shrubs, and small ground-level plants flourish in these clearings.

In the warmer southern areas of taiga, liquid water is available to plants for longer periods of the year. Because of this, the trees grow more densely, producing closed taiga forest. The tree cover is often so thick that only a little light reaches the forest floor.

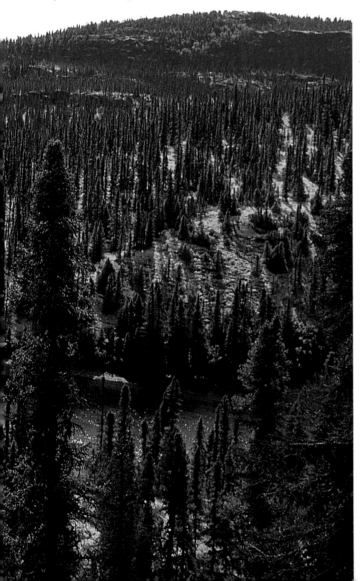

Shrubs and other small plants have limited opportunity to survive here, except where natural clearings are created by fires, fallen trees, or areas of marshy ground.

From Bogs to Forests

Low-lying hollows and depressions in the forest collect water from surrounding areas, and the soil becomes so wet that trees cannot grow at all. In these boggy, airless conditions, the **bacteria** that normally breaks down dead material cannot thrive, so pine needles and other debris that accumulate in the hollow decay very slowly. This creates good conditions for mosses, such as sphagnum. Such mosses change the character of the soil. Over decades, the mosses die away and become sediments that gradually fill the hollows. Eventually, the hollows become dry enough for trees to grow there.

NORTHEASTERN AMERICAN TAIGA

The eastern belt of taiga in North America sprawls across ancient mountains and wet lowlands. The region's landscape, including the immense Hudson Bay, was created by massive glaciers.

The beauty of this lake in Ontario is typical of the hundreds that are scattered through the region. Some of the lakes are popular vacation destinations.

Fact File

▲ More than half of Canada's electricity comes from hydroelectric power stations in the taiga.

▲ Michigan is known as the Wolverine State. Trappers would bring wolverine furs to trading posts in the state. Wolverines are now rare in North America.

▲ Half of Canada's population is clustered in towns and cities around the St. Lawrence River. Farmers have cleared most of the forests along the river.

1. Lake Superior
The world's largest surface area of freshwater. It covers almost the same area as Maine. Invasive zebra mussels outcompete native mussels in the lake.

2. Ouimet Canyon
A sheer gorge 152 meters (500 feet) wide and 107 meters (350 feet) deep.

3. Hudson Bay
This massive bay is ice-locked from November to July.

4. Canadian Shield
A flat area that was once a towering range of mountains.

5. Adirondack Mountains
An area of taiga wilderness popular with hikers. Invasive plants, such as milfoil, have been clogging the waterways and wetlands in recent years.

6. Charlevoix Reserve
A protected region of taiga, broad-leaved forests, and wetlands. The area also contains the 700-meter (2,200-foot) Hautes-Gorges, which are the deepest in eastern Canada.

7. Réservoir Manicouagan
A vast asteroid crater that has been made into the world's sixth-largest reservoir.

8. Acadia National Park
Reserve protecting America's most southerly taiga forest. Infestations of the invasive emerald ash borer beetle are damaging trees in the park.

9. Labrador
A large peninsula in northeastern Canada. Its rugged coast of fjords and islands was formed by glaciers.

10. Newfoundland
The main island in the larger province of the same name, visited by Viking explorers 500 years before Columbus's first voyage to America.

Hudson Bay

Churchill

3

NORTH AMERICA
EUROPE
ASIA
AFRICA
SOUTH AMERICA
AUSTRALIA
ANTARCTICA

Labrador Sea

N

9

NEWFOUNDLAND

Marshy lowlands
ITOBA

C A N A D A

James Bay

4

7

Réservoir Manicouagan

10

St John's

ONTARIO

C a n a d i a n   S h i e l d

QUEBEC

Charlevoix Reserve

Gulf of St. Lawrence

P.E.I

Lake Nipigon

6

NEW BRUNSWICK

St. Lawrence River

2

Ouimet Canyon

Quebec

NOVA SCOTIA

Halifax

! 1

Lake Superior

MAINE

Atlantic Ocean

WISCONSIN

Lake Michigan

Lake Huron

Montreal

! 8

Acadia National Park

MICHIGAN

Ottawa

! 5

VT

Toronto

Lake Ontario

Adirondack Mountains

NH

NEW YORK

MA

Boston

Chicago

Lake Erie

PENNSYLVANIA

NJ

CT RI

IN

OH

ILLINOIS

U N I T E D   S T A T E S

0   350 miles
0   350   kilometers

Developing the Wilderness

In the last 30 years, Canada's national and local governments have had to decide how to best protect the taiga wilderness while providing energy and raw materials for the country's expanding population. Between 1975 and 1990, the Cree and Inuit people around the southern part of Hudson Bay lost 15,500 square kilometers (6,000 square miles) of their land to dams (right) and generating stations to provide power for the provinces of Quebec and Ontario. Since then, plans to further develop the wilderness have been subject to stricter controls.

TAIGA PLANTS

Trees dominate the taiga, but taiga forests do not have the lush diversity of tropical forests. Taiga plants have to live in extreme conditions, and only a few species are strong enough to survive.

Only a few hardy plants live in the taiga. Huge areas might be covered by a few species of trees.

About 2,000 different species of conifer, flowering plants, ferns, and mosses live in the world's taiga forests. This is far fewer than the number of species living in forests in warmer parts of the world. The majority of taiga trees belong to a mere dozen or so species, most of which are **evergreen** conifers with needlelike leaves.

Since the end of the last **ice age**, some 10,000 years ago, **glaciers** have slowly retreated from today's taiga regions. Glaciers still flow through some taiga forests, such as those in parts of Alaska and Norway. Because of the harsh conditions only a few species have evolved to survive there. The present taiga plants and animals only moved in once the ice had retreated.

 Under Threat

The plant life of the taiga is threatened, mainly by human activities, in several ways. Vast areas of forests are cleared each year for logging, especially in Russia and Canada. If all the trees are removed in an area—a procedure known as clear-cutting—the soil runs off into rivers, and trees cannot grow back. The forest is also cleared for mining. Oil, gas, coal, metals, and diamonds are all mined in the taiga. Processing plants for these operations pollute the environment, further affecting wildlife.

Acid rain also damages taiga forests. This is caused by the fumes from factories reacting with water molecules in the atmosphere and falling as rain. Global warming—the gradual warming of the Earth's climate caused by pollutants in the atmosphere—also threatens the forests. As climate warms the taiga may become drier and the damp-loving forest will shift, possibly farther north—to more suitable regions. At present, there are still enormous areas of taiga forest intact and specific plant species are not considered under threat of extinction. However, with continued unsustainable logging, mining, and global warming, many taiga plant species will become rare in the near future.

The needles of a silver fir tree. These waxy spikes stay on the tree all year round and can withstand ice, snow, and high winds.

Life in the Cold

In many parts of the taiga, tree roots cannot penetrate very far into the soil before they reach the rock-solid permafrost. They have to get all their water and nutrients from the top 1 meter (39 inches) or so of soil. During the freezing winters, when liquid water is in very short supply, taiga plants need to hold onto all the water they can get.

The conifers' needlelike leaves have a thick, waxy coating that stops water from leaking out. The coating also acts like a suit of armor, giving the leaf strength. Like the leaves of most large plants, conifer needles absorb the gases they need, and get rid of waste gases, through tiny holes called stomata. Conifer stomata are often sunken into grooves, which avoids their losing too much water while taking in and giving out gases.

Dense taiga forests create their own cushioned environment. The sheltered, shaded conditions trap moist air, reduce wind speeds, and keep temperature changes to a minimum. Most conifers are evergreen—they keep their leaves all year around. They can photosynthesize (trap sunlight to make food) and grow whenever the Sun is shining, although most growing occurs during the short, warm summers. The trees' needles are angled so they can collect sunlight coming from all directions.

Larches survive in the coldest conditions of all. Although they are conifers, they shed their leaves in winter to reduce water loss and frost damage. They have shallow, widespread roots that capture whatever water is available and also anchor the trees in the ground to withstand gales.

 Fact File

▲ In 1915, a fire in Siberia burned an area roughly five times the size of Spain and Portugal.

▲ Trembling and quaking aspens get their name from the quivering effect of the leaves in the breeze.

▲ Many conifer trees are cone-shaped. Heavy snow slides off the downward-sloping branches, so it does not weigh down and damage the tree.

Hidden Partnership

Beneath the forest floor is a complex network of **fungi**, whose threadlike feeding tubes, or **hyphae**, permeate the soil. Hyphae are the underground parts of fungi. We notice the presence of fungi only when they produce mushrooms and toadstools above the surface.

Many fungal hyphae form partnerships with tree roots, entwining around them or even growing inside them. Such partnerships are called **mycorrhizae**. The hyphae in mycorrhizae digest dead matter in the soil, releasing nutrients for both themselves and the tree. Besides providing nutrients, mycorrhizae protect trees from disease and harmful soil bacteria, by producing antibiotics (bacteria-killing substances). In return, trees create the right conditions for mycorrhizae to flourish. They shed dead needles for the fungi to feed on, and their roots provide a supply of sugar. All in all, the partnership works well for both. Without the mycorrhizae, conifer forests would not grow as thickly as they do. Smaller taiga plants, including wildflowers such as orchids, rely on mycorrhizae to survive on the forest floor.

Trees Dominate

For a small plant, it is a tough life trying to grow on the floor of a thick conifer forest. The trees cut out the sunlight, they take water and nutrients from the soil, and they

A rain-covered mushroom sits among spruce saplings. Fungi play a very important role in the life of taiga trees.

This pine drop plant is an unusual species that grows in North American taiga. Pine drops do not photosynthesize but get food by breaking down fallen pine needles.

shed twigs and needles that can smother a growing plant. Worse than that, the needles contain toxic substances that stop other plants from growing nearby. Few plants can thrive under a dense forest canopy. But if a clearing forms when a tree falls over or burns down, smaller plants have a chance to gain a foothold. They grow quickly and spread their seeds before a new tree takes over the space. The seeds lie in the soil waiting for another clearing to open up.

Layer upon Layer

A few shrubs, such as junipers, wild roses, and alders, do grow below the conifer canopy. The shrubs' fruits provide food for forest animals, which may also shelter among the plants' tangled branches.

Lower down at ground level, cowberry, bilberry, and twinflower plants grow in scattered patches, particularly where the tree cover is sparse. Where the soil is damp, lichens and mosses hug the ground. Higher up, other lichens grow on branches and tree trunks wherever the air is clean. Their absence is a sign that the air is polluted.

The plants of the forest floor grow in dim light. In fact, were they to be placed in bright sunlight most would shrivel and die. Some forest-floor plants bear nectar-rich flowers to attract insects to pollinate them. Generally, these plants—cowberries, wintergreens, and starflowers, among them—have white flowers. These are bold signals to attract bees and butterflies in the forest gloom.

Nature's Larder

The seeds and fruits of trees and shrubs are the main food source for many of the taiga's animals, including squirrels and chipmunks, and birds such as nutcrackers and crossbills. Although this seems like bad news for the plants, they, too, can benefit. For example, nutcrackers and crossbills eat the seeds of Swiss stone pine. At least some of the seeds pass through the birds' digestive systems unharmed. When they land on the ground, the birds' droppings provide a helpful dollop of natural fertilizer. Brown bears and capercaillies perform a similar service in spreading juniper and bilberry seeds.

Animals also disperse seeds and fruits without having to eat them. The tiny, spiny fruit of the twinflower catches on the fur of small mammals and the feathers of birds. The animals may travel far and wide before the fruit drops to the ground.

In Death, Life

The thick layer of pine needles on the forest floor takes time to break down. Gradually, the poisons inside the needles are washed out by rain, and the needles become brittle and vulnerable to attack. Armies of small animals, such as springtail insects, soil mites, wood lice, and earthworms, eat the needles and other buried debris. As the plant matter is broken down into smaller and smaller

What Is a Cone?

Most mature conifers produce scaly structures called cones. A cone is a conifer's equivalent to a flower. Male cones tend to be smaller and mature earlier than female cones. They produce pollen grains, which are released into air when the cone's scales open up (right). The pollen is carried on the wind and caught in open female cones. The male and female sex cells fuse inside the female cone and produce seeds. The female cones then close up, and the scales do not open again until the seeds are ripe. The ripe seeds fall out of the cones and drop to the ground or travel on the wind, until they land in a suitable place to grow. The entire breeding process, from the growth of cones to the release of the seeds, takes about 15 months.

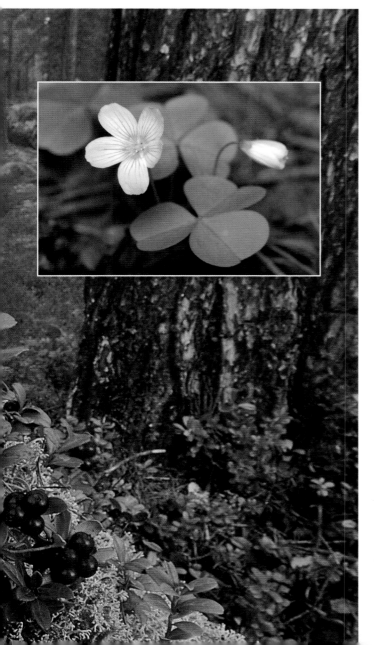

chunks, fungi and bacteria finish off the decaying process that the animals began. The chemicals locked up in the dead plant material are gradually returned to the soil.

Do-It-Yourself

Plants do not always rely on animals to transport pollen, or to scatter fruits and seeds. Many plants are able to produce seeds without having to receive pollen from another plant. For example, the common wood sorrel and May lily produce white flowers to attract insects, but they can pollinate themselves if necessary. They can also produce new plants by growing underground stems that establish independent roots and shoots nearby.

Mosses and Lichens

Mosses carpet the tree trunks and ground in damp taiga. They photosynthesize, but unlike seed-producing plants such as trees and wildflowers, they have no true leaves. Mosses also take up water and nutrients from the soil, but they do not have proper roots. They can reproduce sexually, but they release

The silver fronds growing among this cowberry bush are lichens, confusingly named reindeer moss. Common wood sorrel (inset) grows among the taiga forest understory.

sperm into water, rather than producing pollen grains. The sperm swim to other plants and fertilize their female sex cells. Mosses are simple, miniature plants, but they have some major advantages over larger plants. They can withstand drying out. Some types can lose three-quarters of their water—becoming leathery tufts—but swell up and spring back to life again when water returns. And mosses can absorb water and dissolved minerals directly from snow and rain. They do not need to have roots in the soil.

Lichens are even hardier than mosses. They are a partnership between fungi and **algae** (simple plantlike organisms). The algae photosynthesize and provide food, while the fungi absorb water and minerals from the rain and snow. The fungi also form protective sheaths around the fragile algae. These sheaths shrink and close in dry conditions when water could be lost, and open again when moisture returns. Lichens thrive on moist bark and fallen wood. Beautifully sculpted lichens, such as the fine strands of one

Fire in the Taiga

Fire in taiga forests sounds like bad news, but many of the trees can cope with heat and flames. Larches and pines have thick bark that offers good protection against fire damage. (Spruces and firs, however, tend to have thinner bark and shallow roots that are damaged by fire.) The cones of jack pines release their seeds only after a fire. The heat makes the cones explode, releasing the seeds, which then have a good chance of germinating in the ash-covered clearing created by the fire. Flames and searing heat also sterilize the forest floor and kill off disease-causing organisms and parasites. Fires clear space for new trees to grow (below), and the ash adds nutrients to the soil. Following a fire, a rich variety of small ground plants grow, until the hardy coniferous trees and other taiga plants gradually take over once again.

species named old man's beard, cover branches. Some lichens growing on trees produce acids that have antibiotic properties. They may even protect their host trees from attacks by wood-destroying fungi.

Dark Conifers

The dark conifers—the spruces and firs—are so-called because their leaves are very dark green. When seen from an aircraft, these trees darken large areas of forest. In European taiga, Norway spruce is the most common species. In Asia, the Siberian spruce is the dominant dark conifer.

Taiga Plants of North America

The trees that grow in the North American taiga are typical of taiga around the world. Hardy larches survive in the far north. Spruces and firs cover the main parts of the region, while deciduous trees, such as birches, become more common farther south. The coastal forests of giant redwood trees, however, are unique. No other taiga gets so much rain, and these forests are lusher than in other areas.

Larch trees live at the northern edge of taiga.

Black spruces grow in cold conditions.

Douglas firs are common in mountain forest.

Paper birches are deciduous trees that live in southern taiga.

Redwoods, the world's largest trees, grow in forests along the coast of the Pacific Northwest.

Mosses grow best in damp places. In the Hoh Rain Forest in Washington State, mosses almost completely cover the trees, thanks to the high rainfall.

Spruces are slow-growing and need damp soil all year around. In winter, these trees look particularly attractive because the pale snow contrasts heavily with their dark foliage. In Nordic folklore, spruce forests are said to be the home of mischievous gnomes, goblins, and trolls.

In North America, the black (or bog) spruce is a common dark conifer. These trees are generally small and hardy and grow in very cold and boggy conditions. The white spruce is a taller dark conifer that grows in warmer, better-drained soil in the region.

Fir trees do not grow as far north as spruces. They require milder conditions and more fertile soils. The Douglas fir of North America is one of the world's largest trees, reaching 100 meters (330 feet) in height, with a trunk 5 meters (16 feet) across. They form forests in the Rocky Mountains and grow in mixed forests close to the Pacific Northwest coast.

 ## Christmas Trees

In Europe and North America, people buy conifers to decorate their homes at Christmas. Different species are chosen in different countries, depending on availability and local preferences. In North America, for example, the Douglas fir is popular; in parts of Europe, Norway spruce is the favorite.

The link between conifers and Christmas goes back more than 1,000 years. According to tradition, St. Boniface, an English missionary in Germany in the 8th century C.E., stumbled across people worshipping an oak tree dedicated to the god Thor. In anger, Boniface cut down the tree, and a fir tree began to grow in its place. Since then, fir trees have been linked with Christian worship.

Light Conifers

Light conifers have paler leaves and include most pines and larches. They are more widely distributed than dark conifers because they can tolerate a broader range of conditions. The Scotch pine is the most common light conifer, covering much of the European and Asian taiga. In North America, jack pine

This patch of southern forest taiga has both evergreen and deciduous trees. The deciduous aspen trees have shed their leaves, while the conifers (rear) keep their needles.

takes the lead. Larches are light conifers that shed their leaves. They can resist extreme cold and grow farther north than any other type of tree.

Deciduous Trees

A few deciduous trees, which shed leaves in winter, grow in taiga. Birches, aspens, and poplars grow in warmer, southern regions. European white birch and trembling aspen grow in Europe and Asia, and white birch and quaking aspen live in North America.

EUROPEAN TAIGA

The European taiga grows right across the continent from Scotland to the Urals of Russia. In western Europe, taiga forests grow around lakes and wetlands. In the east, the forest covers a huge, featureless lowland.

 Fact File

▲ Russia is in both Europe and Asia and is the world's largest country.

▲ About three-quarters of Finland is covered in forest and woodland.

▲ The Swedes and Finns manage their forests so that timber is not cut down faster than it is replaced.

▲ The biggest threats to the taiga are logging and exploration and extraction of oil and gas.

Background: An open forest in Lapland in northern Sweden. Lapland is home to the Sami people and spreads across the whole of northern Scandinavia.

Climate Change

People were living in northern taiga forests 100,000 years ago. But when the last ice age began about 70,000 years ago, the world cooled and glaciers spread as far south as Italy. The ice sheet forced the taiga south as well, and animals that were adapted to live in cold conditions, such as woolly mammoths (right), lived in regions that are now noted for their warm weather. The people of the taiga also moved south as the forests shifted. Today, the ice has retreated north, and taiga grows in its current location.

1. Scotland
Scottish taiga is scattered in small patches. Tree-felling, followed by sheep- and deer-grazing, have removed most of the original forest.

2. Sweden
Until the 1990s, Swedish conifers were badly affected by acid rain created by pollution from Great Britain and Germany. Stricter controls have since been brought in to protect forests.

3. Kaliningrad
This ancient seaport on the Baltic Sea is now part of an isolated Russian enclave. The sea is very polluted from industries and sewage.

4. Stabbursdalen
The Gulf Stream warms the climate of this Norwegian national park. Taiga forest grows farther north here than anywhere else on Earth.

5. Pyhä-Häkki
A protected area of peatland and forest with centuries-old trees.

6. St. Petersburg, Russia
Called Leningrad during the communist era, this is Russia's largest seaport. The city is a major source of sea pollution.

7. Karelia
This region has the most diverse taiga forests and wetlands in Europe.

8. Lake Ladoga
At 18,100 square kilometers (7,000 square miles), this is the largest lake in Europe. Overfishing and pollution are problems in the lake.

9. Kola Peninsula
This part of Scandinavia is in Russia. It is an important mining center and has several hydroelectric plants along its fast-flowing rivers. Wastes from nuclear industries affect sealife.

10. Volga River
The Volga, flowing 3,530 kilometers (2,193 miles), is the longest river in Europe. It empties into the Caspian Sea in Russia. Parts of the river are polluted.

11. Pechoro-Ilychskiy Nature Reserve
This reserve—at 2,656 square kilometers (6,880 square miles) —is mostly covered in forest.

12. Ural Mountains
The Ural Mountains separate Europe from Asia. The region is rich in metals such as copper and gold. Mining and drilling have an impact on wildlife.

TAIGA ANIMALS

Despite the long months of snow and ice, a wide variety of animals eke out an existence in taiga forests, including some of the world's largest land animals. Most live alone among the forest trees, rarely crossing each other's path.

The long, hard winter of the taiga presents a great challenge for most animals living there. Thick snow makes it difficult for larger animals to move about, and the snow covers food on the ground.

Most of the large animals of the taiga feed on plant material, such as leaves, fruit, and seeds. In the long winter, deer have to exist on tree bark, mosses, and lichens. Chipmunks, woodmice, and squirrels rely on hidden stores of seeds and summer fruits.

As for the smallest creatures, such as insects and other invertebrates, many live underneath tree bark, among the leaf litter, and buried in the soil. In winter, the adults of some species hide away in a **dormant** (inactive) state. For other species only the eggs or young forms survive until spring. Some of these animals have natural antifreeze in their body fluids.

In summer, taiga forests are filled with biting insects. The insects spend the winter as dormant pupae and develop into adults as the warm weather begins.

Moose are at home in shallow water (right), where they feed on soft aquatic plants. In winter these large deer eat less, surviving mainly on bark.

This substance stops them from freezing to death. Most taiga invertebrates feed on detritus—the dead remains of plants and animals. Others feed on the heartwood of trees, deep inside their trunks.

Because the taiga is so cold, and conifer needles contain many waxy and toxic substances, dead plant matter takes a long time to break down. In summer, an army of slugs, millipedes, woodlice, and beetles feeds on the decomposing plant matter. As they break it down, they release nutrients and return them to the soil.

Eaten Alive

At the height of the short summer, taiga forests are filled with flying insects, many of which bite larger animals. The air is alive with millions of mosquitoes and blackflies feasting on the blood of **mammals**—including

When Big Is Best

In a cold environment, large size can be an advantage. The ratio of body surface area to weight of most large animals is less than that of smaller animals. This means that for their weight, large animals have a relatively smaller area of skin through which they lose heat, which their bodies have generated. They are therefore better at keeping warm. This is why male stoats from northern Canada weigh about three times as much as their cousins in milder forests in the United States. It also helps explain why many taiga animals are record breakers: The moose is the world's largest deer, the wolverine the largest weasel, and bears (right) are the largest land predators.

Wolves spend the winter living in packs. They hunt as a team, traveling large distances in pursuit of their prey. In summer the packs disband, and wolves may hunt alone.

people. Only the female flies feed on blood—to provide enough energy to produce their eggs. The males eat flower nectar and plant sap. Mosquitoes lay their eggs in water, where their larvae hatch and grow. If the summer is particularly dry, there will be far fewer mosquitoes than usual. A warm, wet summer, however, is good for mosquitoes.

Deer

Moose and caribou are the taiga's largest plant eaters. Caribou, which are named reindeer in Europe and Siberia, migrate from tundra to taiga in winter, but moose—known as elk outside of North America—tend to remain in the taiga all year round.

The moose is lord of the taiga and the world's largest species of deer. Males are more than 1.8 meters (6 feet) tall at the shoulder and can weigh 500 kilograms (1,100 pounds). Despite their large size, moose are shy and peaceful animals. With keen senses of smell and hearing, they generally disappear into the forest when disturbed. Nevertheless, if confronted, a moose can defend itself well. Using antlers reaching up to 2 meters (79 inches) across, and kicking with its sharp hooves, a healthy adult male can fend off all but the worst wolf attacks. However, the males use their antlers more often in ritual fights with rivals over access to female mates.

Moose prefer to graze on the leaves and fruit of small plants at the edges of the forest and in clearings. They have a large appetite and can eat around 15 kilograms (33 pounds) of food a day in winter and an incredible 35 kilograms (77 pounds) daily in summer.

These deer spend long periods close to ponds and rivers, because there are plenty of edible plants in the water and along the banks. In summer they sometimes submerge themselves for hours on end, to avoid the swarms of biting insects. The water is also a haven from marauding wolves. In winter,

with food very scarce, moose eat strips of tree bark. A large population of moose can devastate forests this way.

Wood bison live in the southern parts of the North American taiga. These very rare animals are not deer but are closely related to the cattlelike bison that once lived in huge herds in the open prairies to the south.

Pack Hunters

Unlike all other taiga **predators**, gray wolves hunt cooperatively. In deep winter, when food is scarce, they gather together to track and overpower even the largest deer. In summer they are more likely to hunt separately, going after much smaller prey, such as squirrels and marmots.

 A Pale Shadow

Thick fur or feathers keep many taiga animals warm in winter. Some of the taiga's mammals—the snowshoe hare and the stoat (below), for instance—turn white in winter. This change of color serves as camouflage in a snow-covered landscape, allowing the hare to hide from predators more easily, and the stoat to sneak up on its victims. Pale fur may offer better insulation than dark fur. Some scientists believe that dark pigment (colored chemical) thickens the hair. Pale fur is thinner, leaving more space between the hairs to trap warm air, and this improves insulation.

The female capercaillie (bird on left) is smaller and less conspicuous than the male. The males use their distinctive plumage in complex displays to attract mates.

The wolf pack—a family group of 8 to 12 wolves led by a single male and female pair—tracks its quarry by smell. Wolves can smell their prey from more than 1.6 kilometers (1 mile) away. Once they pick up a scent, they cluster together—almost like football players in a huddle—before setting off in pursuit. What messages they pass to one another at this time—by growls, a flick of the ear, a shake of the head—are still a mystery.

Once the wolves get close to their prey, they begin the attack. The onslaught is triggered by the victim fleeing in fright. The wolves take turns jumping onto the prey, inflicting bites that injure and gradually weaken it. Little by little, the panic-stricken animal is overpowered and then torn to pieces. Each wolf gobbles down as much meat as it can manage. Adult wolves can gorge 9 kilograms (20 pounds) at a single sitting.

Threatened Taiga Animals

Many taiga animals are in decline. The main reasons for this are habitat loss and hunting. Although only a few species are threatened with extinction, the numbers of taiga animals are dwindling in the southern taiga, where most human activity, such as hunting and logging, takes place. Siberian tigers and snow leopards have been hunted by humans for centuries because they prey on livestock. Wolverines were once common in the United States but are now rarely seen there.

In many areas, populations of animals have become extinct. For example, wolves and bears are now extinct in the United Kingdom. Beavers have been reintroduced in some parts of the world where they used to live. There are pros and cons for this reintroduction. Although they enrich the environment by creating fertile meadows within forests, beavers make dams that can flood farmland. The capercaillie—the largest member of the grouse family—died out in Scotland in the 18th century because of hunting. It was reintroduced in the 19th century from Sweden but is now struggling to survive mainly because of lack of suitable habitat.

In certain areas of the taiga, such as parks and reserves, the animals are protected from uncontrolled hunting and logging. But little of the taiga is protected. There are breeding programs for Siberian tigers and snow leopards, but these captive animals do not develop the hunting skills necessary to survive in the wild. One success story is the wood bison. This close relative of the plains bison, commonly known as buffalo, lives in the taiga forests of Canada. Once severely hunted, it is now protected, and its numbers have risen from about 200 in the 1950s to about 3,000 today.

Summer Visitors

The arrival of spring in the taiga fills the air with birdsong. Many of the taiga's birds, such as Siberian rubythroats, are summer visitors. They fly north to take advantage of the abundant insect life on the trees, in the air, and on the ground. Many birds nest in taiga forest trees, raise their young, and then fly south to spend the winter in warmer areas.

Taiga Fighter

Few birds remain in the taiga all year round. Among those that do are woodpeckers, crossbills, nuthatches, and, biggest of all, the

Despite their reputation and bloodthirsty hunting techniques, wolves are really timid creatures. There are few, if any, properly documented examples of wolves attacking and killing people. In fact, people are a much bigger danger to wolves than the other way around. Hunters shooting wolves over the last 200 years have massively reduced wolf numbers around the world.

The Siberian crane raises its chicks in the marshes of the Russian taiga. The survival of this rare bird is threatened by hunters and habitat loss.

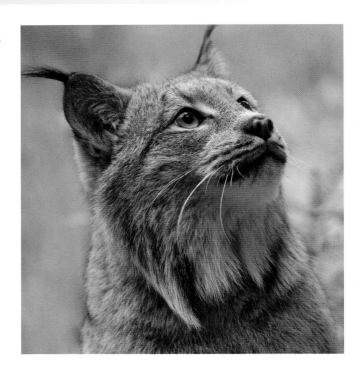

Canadian lynx are found in North America, and Eurasian lynx in Europe and Asia. Their ranges extend into taiga forests, where these medium-sized cats hunt hares, rodents, birds, fish, and sometimes deer.

capercaillie. This bulky bird, a type of grouse weighing up to 6 kilograms (13 pounds), feeds on wild fruits in summer and fall and resorts to a diet of pine needles in winter. In the cold season, capercaillies stay in trees during the day and bury themselves in snow to pass the night. In the summer a male capercaillie stridently defends his territory against other males. When a resident male spots another male approaching, he gives a call that sounds a little like a cork being pulled from a bottle. If the call has no effect, the defending male drops to the ground and prepares to fight the invader. The fight begins as a ritual in which the birds pretend to bite each other. If one does not back down, the confrontation can degenerate into a brawl, with one bird clasping the neck of the other. If the males are well matched, they fight until one is seriously injured or dead. The winner controls the territory and has access to females.

Head-Bangers

The black woodpecker is the largest and loudest woodpecker in Europe and Asia. It uses its chisel-like beak to excavate holes in tree trunks and pry off bark to reveal hidden

Beavers are large rodents that build dams and homes called lodges from tree branches. They gnaw through tree trunks with their sharp front teeth. Their ranges include the taiga forests of North America and Europe.

Hunting in the Snow

In winter much of the taiga is covered in snow around 90 centimeters (3 feet) deep, and temperatures plunge to −40°C (−40°F). The small forest predators hunt beneath the snow. There, weasels and stoats pursue shrews and rodents, such as squirrels. Shrews, in turn, hunt insects, while the rodents search for pine cones.

Large animals have difficulty moving through the deep snow. The exceptions are wolverines, which have broad feet that act like snowshoes. The wolverine's dense, long fur is another aid in icy weather. It does not freeze, even when wet.

The wolverine of North America (below)—known as a glutton in Europe and Asia—belongs to the weasel family. It has a remarkable reputation for strength and aggressiveness, out of all proportion to its size. Although it grows to only 27 kilograms (60 pounds) in weight, a wolverine can take on a caribou or moose floundering in deep snow. Sometimes a wolverine stumbles through a camper's tent, trashing the contents along the way.

Wolverines are solitary animals, except during the brief breeding season. In summer, they eat small rodents, eggs, young birds, and insects, supplemented with wild fruits and pine seeds. They also eat carrion, sometimes following wolf packs to scavenge for scraps left behind. Wolverines have even been known to drive bears from their kills.

People rarely see wolverines because they are mostly active at night, and trapping and hunting have severely reduced their numbers. Females give birth to two or three cubs in mid to late winter, safe within a den under snow and often beneath a fallen tree. The young can hunt for themselves by the end of their first summer.

European Taiga Animals

Fewer species of large animals live in taiga than in other biomes. Many of these animals spend long periods without seeing another member of their own species. Despite being small in number, these species are spread over a wide area. Many, such as wolves and bears, live in all parts of the biome and also reside south of the taiga belt. Caribou and bears spend the summer in barren tundra to the north of the taiga.

 Moose, or elk. Most common in Scandinavia.

 Gray wolf. Lives in packs in most parts of taiga.

 Black woodpecker. The largest woodpecker in the region.

 Caribou, or reindeer. Spends winter in taiga.

 Brown bear. A large, solitary omnivore.

 Wolverine. A large, weasel-like predator.

insects. It is not unusual for these voracious birds to eat a thousand ants or beetle larvae (young) during a single meal.

The holes these woodpeckers make provide homes for other creatures, from owls to red squirrels, and by breaking up rotten wood, the birds speed up the recycling of nutrients. Black woodpeckers have a remarkable tongue that extends more than 5 centimeters (2 inches) beyond its bill. It is pointed and covered in hooklike barbs that stick into food.

Like other woodpeckers, the birds' brains are cushioned by a sac of fluid enclosed within a thick skull. These structures absorb the thousands of blows delivered by the bird's bill each day. The sound of a woodpecker's drilling can be heard well over a kilometer away.

Nutcrackers and Crossbills

Some birds are highly dependent on the seeds of conifer trees. Nutcrackers use their powerful beaks to crush and batter pine and spruce cones, releasing the seeds. Crossbills are more delicate—they pry open the cones to extract the seeds. Different species of crossbills have beaks suited to particular types of cones. In Siberia, the parrot crossbill uses a robust, rounded beak to extract seeds from tough pine cones, while the two-barred crossbill, with a thinner bill, goes for the more delicate cones of the larch.

Almost all taiga birds breed in spring and summer when food is plentiful. Crossbills, however, breed during winter. They are able to breed at this time because they have a plentiful year-round source of seeds. Nutcrackers breed in spring. In fall, they bury supplies of seeds under the snow to see them through the hard times ahead.

Voles

Forest voles are tiny rodents, with adults weighing only about 40 grams (1.5 ounces). They avoid the worst of the winter by digging tunnels in snow; the air-filled snow is a good insulator against the cold weather outside. Under the snow, voles search for buried nuts and soft fruits. In summer, their diet is much more varied, including seeds, leaves, mushrooms, soft fruits, lichens, bark, and insects. Like most rodents, they can breed quickly when conditions are favorable, producing up to five litters a year.

Squirrels

Squirrels and chipmunks eat pine nuts and bury cones in a winter food store. Red squirrels use their sharp incisor teeth to gnaw the scales off spruce and pine cones to get at the seeds. They are active almost all year round and keep moving during summer, searching for fresh cones. In winter, they rely on food they have buried. A red squirrel may bury 200 cones in a day. Uneaten seeds begin growing into trees the following spring.

Crossbills are so called because the tips of their bills cross over like a pair of scissors. This helps them snip into cones to get at the seeds inside.

Miniature Carnivores

Stoats and weasels are the small predators of the taiga—long, sleek, and agile, they are rarely more than 24 centimeters (9 inches) from head to tail and weigh less than 200 grams (7 ounces). The stoat—with its pale, thick winter coat—was a favorite quarry of trappers. The pale winter fur, called ermine, was used for making ceremonial robes. In 1937, Canada exported 50,000 ermine pelts to Britain for the coronation of King George VI. Some 300 pelts were needed to make a single gown. Stoats mate during the summer, but the babies do not develop inside the females' womb until many months later.

A hoary marmot keeps a lookout for danger in an Alaskan forest clearing. These large rodents give a range of alarm calls when they spot predators.

This delays pregnancy and so ensures that young are born the following spring, after the thaw, when food is easier to find.

Silent but Deadly

The great gray owl of the Russian taiga looks much larger than its true body size because of its thick downy feathers. These are good for keeping out the cold, but they also dampen any sounds during flight. The owl hunts by listening for the delicate scratchings of its

Bear Feast

Fast, cold rivers flow through the taiga of Europe and North America. In some of these rivers, once a year a miraculous fishing event takes place. Salmon, fresh from the sea where they have been fattening themselves for several years, fight their way upriver to spawn (lay eggs). They battle to overcome all obstacles in their path—including waterfalls and fishing nets—in their desire to reach the spawning grounds. Salmon return to the very same stretches of river where they themselves hatched from eggs many years before. Predators, especially bears, relish this annual bonanza.

In the taiga forests of Canada and Russia, brown bears wait in the shallows at the base of rapids (below left). Here, salmon gather before their fight upstream. The fish sometimes pack so densely that the bears just have to scoop their paws through the water to catch one.

For the chinook salmon of Alaska and northern Canada, spawning ends in the exhausted adults' death. Their decaying bodies fertilize the river water, encouraging plankton and plants to grow, and in turn small freshwater animals, such as insect larvae. The newly hatched salmon feed on these creatures.

prey—generally voles. Once located, the owl hovers above and then drops onto its prey, which may be deep below the snow. The owl plunges through the snow, seizes the victim in its talons, and kills it with a bite to the back of the neck.

Coping with Winter

Many taiga animals spend the cold winter inside warm nests in an inactive state. They eat as much as they can during the short summer and put on fat reserves to last them through winter. Nevertheless, many rely on food stores during the cold season. The Siberian chipmunk, for example, often leaves its nest to feast on its seed store.

Only a few taiga animals, such as the squirrel-like marmot, **hibernate**. They become dormant for long periods, their pulse and breathing rates drop to a fraction of their normal level, and they do not feed. Even so, they wake every few weeks to get rid of urine, and they stir during the coldest spells to avoid freezing to death. Contrary to popular belief, bears are not true hibernators. They do not sleep right through the winter, but wake up at intervals. A mother brown bear, for example, wakes regularly to suckle her cubs.

SIBERIAN TAIGA

The Siberian taiga is the world's largest forest, covering an area twice that of the Amazon rain forest. It is crossed by some of the world's biggest rivers, down which timber companies float felled logs to sawmills and factories.

A village in western Siberia. Millions of Russians have moved into the taiga in the last 300 years.

Kara Sea

Gulf of Ob

NORTH AMERICA

SOUTH AMERICA

EUROPE

AFRICA

ASIA

AUSTRALIA

ANTARCTICA

Igar

Ob River

West Siberian Plain

 1

Omsk

To

Novosibirsk

KAZAKHSTAN

Siberia Facts

▲ The Ural Mountains stop rain clouds from reaching western Siberia. To the east of the mountains the climate tends to be dry with bitterly cold winters and hot summers.

▲ The Trans-Siberian Railroad crosses seven different time zones.

▲ The Siberian taiga is bordered by the arctic tundra on the north and the Kazakh and Mongolian steppes (grasslands) in the south.

Laptev Sea

RUSSIA

N

Khatanga River

Anabar River

Olenëk River

Central Siberian Plateau

Lena River

Lower Tunguska River

Vilyuy River

[2] ⊙

[3] Central Siberian Biosphere Reserve

Yenisey River

[5] Tunguska Event

Stony Tunguska River

Lena River

Angara River

Stolbies

[4]

Bratsk Reservoir

Yablonovyy Mountains

Lake Baikal

• Krasnoyarsk

⊙ [6]

Irkutsk

[7]

CHINA

Sayanskiy Mountains

0   200 miles
0   200   kilometers

1. Ob River
The Ob flows from the Altai Mountains close to the Mongolian border to the Gulf of Ob in the Arctic. Pollution in the river has reduced fish stocks.

2. Yenisey River
This river is an important transportation route. Timber is shipped around the world from Igarka in the northwest. Pollution from oil and gas extraction is a problem in the river.

3. Central Siberian Biosphere Reserve
A large taiga reserve in the homeland of the Evenki people, who carry on their traditional way of life.

4. Stolbies
Unique volcanic-rock formations created by wind and rain. Many stolbies are contained in a taiga nature reserve beside the Yenisey River. The tallest reaches 120 meters (395 feet) high.

5. Tunguska Event
On June 30, 1908, a comet or meteoroid exploded 5–10 kilometers (3.2–6.2 miles) in the air near the Stony Tunguska River. More than 2,150 square kilometers (830 square miles) of forest was destroyed, and, hundreds of miles away, trains were derailed by the impact.

6. Lake Baikal
Lake Baikal covers one and a half times the area of New Jersey. The lake holds the largest volume of freshwater of any lake in the world. In places, it is more than a 1.6 kilometers (1 mile) deep. It harbors 1,500 unique plants and animals, including freshwater seals. Pollution is a problem in parts of the lake.

7. Trans-Siberian Railroad
Along its 9,299-kilometer (5,778-mile) route, from Moscow to Vladivostok, this railroad crosses desert, mountain, and forest. Express trains take seven days to travel its length.

Hidden Wealth

[7]

Much of Russia's wealth lies beneath the taiga of Siberia. Most of Russia's petroleum oil and gas is drilled in western Siberia, while eastern Siberia sits upon huge coal deposits. Siberia's wood and coal are transported long distances to reach industrial centers in European Russia. Most of Siberia's rivers run into the Arctic Ocean and are often blocked by ice. The Trans-Siberian Railroad (right), completed in 1904, is the main transportation link for Siberia's produce.

PEOPLE AND THE TAIGA

With little land suitable for agriculture or industry, the taiga has largely escaped the ravages of the modern world. In the past, people survived mainly by hunting, fishing, and herding caribou.

Compared to other land biomes, the human invasion of the taiga was slow, because the forests are so dense and the weather so extreme. The first people to live in taiga arrived by boat, traveling along major rivers, such as the Lena, Ob, and Yenisey in Siberia, and the Mackenzie and Yukon in North America.

Archeological evidence shows that people have lived in the taiga forests of Asia and Europe for more than 100,000 years. During ice ages throughout this period, ice sheets shifted south as the world cooled. The ice covered the land where taiga forests currently grow, and the biome was positioned farther south than it is now. Each time the world warmed up again, the forests shifted north as the ice sheets melted away.

Over many thousands of years, people moved north and south with the gradual shifts of the taiga, and they were joined by new peoples, who migrated into the area from other biomes.

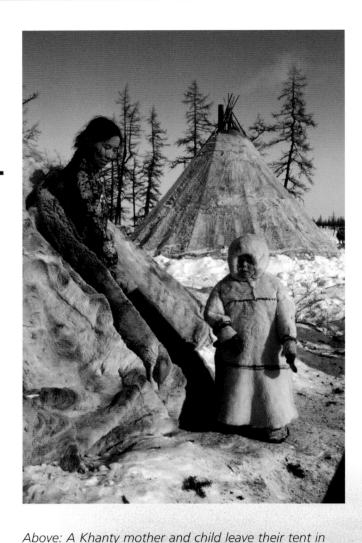

Above: A Khanty mother and child leave their tent in a summer camp in the taiga of European Russia. The Khanty spend the summer on the move with their herds.

People of the European and Asian taiga and tundra may well have been the first to colonize the Americas around 30,000 years ago, when people crossed a strip of land that once existed between Siberia and Alaska. Called the Bering Bridge, this land has since disappeared under the sea.

Siberian Hunters

Around 2,000 years ago, many of the peoples of the Siberian taiga, who had survived by hunting, began to raise herds of caribou. They led a **nomadic** lifestyle, riding the deer or using them for carrying loads. The Evenki people of eastern Siberia would even hunt on deerback.

Nomadic people move from place to place in search of food and water. They must carry their homes with them or hastily construct shelters from natural materials when they arrive at a new campsite. The Khanty people of northern Russia, for example, dig caves in the snow and cover the entrance with animal skins. In summer, some people make temporary tentlike shelters from poles covered in animal skin or birch bark.

Fishers

Some European and Asian taiga peoples, including the Khanty, depended more on fishing than hunting. They led a more settled way of life than hunting people. In winter, they often came together in settlements of 150–170 people. They stored food at the settlement and went on short hunting expeditions in small family groups. When summer arrived, the families would leave for their fishing sites. Typically, one site supported two or three families.

Native Americans

Much less is known about the history of Native American taiga peoples before European settlers arrived. However, some early American history has been passed on in artwork, fables, and folklore.

Below: A herd of caribou is driven through taiga forest in Siberia. These deer are used by many taiga peoples for food, transportation, and clothing.

People probably began to **colonize** the present expanse of North American taiga about 12,000 years ago, as Earth warmed after the last ice age. These people were ancestors of the **Algonquians** and **Athabascans**—two major groups originally from Asia, with different languages. Algonquians live in much of the eastern part of North America. The taiga-dwelling Algonquians live in the area of the Great Lakes, Hudson Bay, and eastern Canada. The Athabascans live in Alaska, along the Pacific coast of North America, and in the Rocky Mountains.

Both groups were hunters and fishers. Men hunted caribou and moose and fished the rivers and lakes. Women and men gathered

A totem pole, topped by an eagle sculpture, stands in the steep mountainous taiga forests of British Columbia.

The members of a family of Alaskan Athabascans display the furs skinned from the animals they have trapped over the long taiga winter.

 Nothing Wasted

The Nenet people of northern Siberia are caribou herders. They live in wood-framed, conical tents covered with caribou hide. Each family looks after a herd of about 70–100 caribou, and when a deer is slaughtered, almost nothing is wasted. The Nenet eat deer meat, drink the deer's blood, and use deer fat for cooking, fuel, and waterproofing. The skin is made into clothes (the word *parka* comes from the Nenet language) and shoes. The Nenet use deer tendons and sinews as sewing threads, and they carve antlers into attractive decorations or make them into tools. There are about 40,000 Nenets in Siberia today.

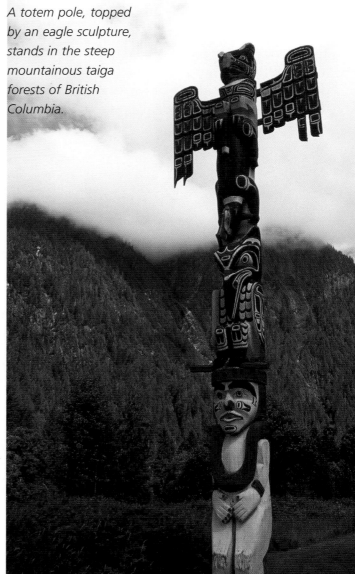

wild fruits, nuts, and roots to supplement their diet of meat. In summer, communities tended to settle near lakes and rivers. In winter, they lived on the move, following the migrating caribou.

Totems

According to the spiritual traditions of many taiga peoples, several forest animals were sacred. Each clan believed it was descended from a particular type of animal, and these animals became revered emblems, or totems. Clan members believed it was wrong to hunt these sacred animals.

Among many Athabascan tribes, the wolf was a totem. It was forbidden to kill wolves, even if they had been attacking caribou herds. They believed that if a wolf was killed, the spirit world would take revenge and send more and more wolves to attack the herds.

The residents of taiga towns live close to nature. This moose is paying a visit to a home in Anchorage, Alaska.

Tribes on the Canadian west coast made totem poles—ornately carved wooden poles ranging from 1.8 meters (6 feet) to 16 meters (50 feet) tall. The poles served different functions: to ward off evil spirits, to honor certain animals, or to record a clan's history.

The Modern Russian Taiga

Russians began migrating into the taiga forests east of the Ural Mountains in the 16th century. People cleared the forest around small settlements to make way for farms. Peasants from eastern Europe settled across the region to escape hardship and poverty in their own countries, and they lived fairly peacefully alongside the native taiga peoples. Siberia became a favored place for Russian governments to send political rebels and criminals. Joseph Stalin, the tyrannical Russian leader, created an enormous network of prison camps there.

Today, most people living in the Siberian taiga are Russians or Ukrainians, rather than historical taiga peoples. They live in cities, such as Irkutsk, Tomsk, and Yakutsk.

Taiga Medicine

Across the taiga of North America, Europe, and Asia, people use more than a thousand species of plants for medicines. Many fruits—among them gooseberries, cowberries, and the fruits of magnolia—contain chemicals that have a stimulant effect. The fruits are consumed for several reasons, including improved blood flow and to stave off fatigue and hunger.

Traditionally, taiga peoples used extracts from a wide range of conifers to treat wounds and skin rashes. The Tanaina of northwest Canada make a tea from juniper branches to treat colds and pneumonia. Sphagnum moss from peat bogs has both antiseptic and absorbent properties. Native North Americans even used it to make diapers.

In Russia, chemicals from ginseng roots (right) were taken to produce a feeling of well-being. Ginseng is now a popular complementary medicine across Europe, America, and China.

North American Taiga Today

Europeans began to colonize North America's taiga in the 17th century, with British people settling in the Hudson Bay region, and the French in Labrador and the St. Lawrence River valley. In 1867, the United States purchased Alaska, originally colonized by Russia, for just $7.2 million—roughly 5 cents a hectare (2 cents an acre). A rich mix of people from Europe and Asia, as well as native descendants, live in Alaska today.

Most early colonizers began trading with Native American peoples of the taiga, but then, to a greater or lesser extent, exploited them and forced them to change their way of life. Today, about 30,000 people of Athabascan descent live in the taiga of Alaska, and northwest and central Canada. They include Tanaina, Tana, and Chippewa tribes. To the east, among the 100,000 people of Algonquian descent that live in taiga

regions, most belong to the Cree, who are historically hunters of caribou and moose. In European colonial days, the Cree traded with both British and French immigrants.

A few residents of the taiga, particularly those in more remote areas, still live a partly nomadic hunting and fishing lifestyle. Others are found on reservations and carry on a traditional way of life, living in tents. However, most native people have abandoned their previous lifestyles and adopted modern urban lives. They still retain their ethnic identity through clothing and art, by practicing traditional crafts, and by partaking in dances and religious ceremonies.

A Hard Life

Living in the taiga has never been easy. Native peoples of the taiga were tough: The women gave birth by the campfire in freezing conditions while on the move from one hunting area to another. The newborn child was rubbed in snow before being held to the mother's breast. Even today, many taiga peoples live without benefit of local medical facilities. In the Siberian taiga, for example, the death rate among young babies is twice that of the Russian average.

Since the 1600s, greater contact with outsiders brought new diseases, such as smallpox, measles, influenza, and tuberculosis, to which taiga peoples had little or no immunity. Colonizers also introduced alcohol. Many taiga peoples—for whom alcoholic drinks have never been a part of their culture—lack the enzyme that breaks down alcohol within the body. For them, drinking alcohol has a far greater intoxicating effect.

A young Mansi man rides through a river in the Ural Mountains of central Russia. Taiga peoples are finding it harder to maintain their way of life.

New diseases, exploitation by outsiders, and the introduction of alcohol and drugs are among the many challenges taiga peoples have had to face. Nevertheless, in many native communities there is renewed awareness of the need to protect traditional values, customs, and ways of life.

Modern Hunting

The taiga's original peoples hunted animals in a sustainable way, so that local populations were not depleted. Since the 16th century, things have changed dramatically.

In the late 1500s, Russians began to colonize the Siberian taiga. The rising demand for fur sent hunters and trappers into the taiga in search of the valuable furs of foxes, beavers, minks, and sables. Rivalry between the French and British over fur-rich territory in eastern Canada led to several wars in the region, with Native Americans fighting on both sides.

Fact File

▲ Present-day Siberian reindeer herders kill up to 20 deer a year to feed and clothe their families.

▲ Thirteen square kilometers (5 square miles) of taiga forest produces enough food for just a single person.

▲ Canada is the world's biggest exporter of wood pulp, which is used to make paper.

▲ Today, most of Canada's furs come from fur farms.

By the 19th century, decades of hunting and trapping had massively reduced the populations of fur-bearing animals in the central and eastern parts of the North American taiga. Then, in the 1840s, the European demand for fur products dropped, as fur clothes became less fashionable. In the late 19th century, the Canadian government bought the land owned by the Hudson Bay Company and began controlling fur hunting.

Modern hunting methods—using high-power rifles and snowmobiles—are so efficient that, even in hostile terrain, local populations of rare fur animals can be wiped out quickly. Today, in many parts of taiga, there are bans on hunting sables, beavers, moose, and some other types of deer.

Logging

Clear-felling—cutting down all the trees in an area of forest—began hundreds of years ago in the taiga of Scandinavia and Russia to supply wood for building ships. From the 1600s onward, loggers in parts of Sweden and Finland also felled trees to provide fuel for the iron industry. Now, little of the original forest remains. However, by the late 1800s, the Scandinavians found that felled conifer forest could regrow, given the chance. This was a better option than turning the land over to farming. The Canadians learned from the Scandinavian experience, and by the late 1870s, they began replanting some of their felled conifer forests.

Clear-felling can cause problems. In the Russian taiga, some felled areas have turned into bog. On slopes, clear-felling can lead to

A clear-felled stretch of taiga cuts through the mature forest. Conifer trees quickly repopulate clear-felled areas, but environmental damage still occurs.

Birch-Bark Canoes

Native Americans of the Canadian northeast used the bark of the white birch to makes canoes (left). They stretched sheets of bark over a cedar frame, sewing them into place with the pliable roots of white spruce. Holes were sewed up and waterproofed with pine resins. The canoes were very light, with a flat bottom, and hunters could easily carry them around obstacles in a river, as they hunted for caribou or moose.

soil erosion, causing nearby rivers to fill with silt. Logjams add to the problem, blocking rivers. This has happened in some parts of European Russia and Siberia. Meanwhile, any remaining soil cover may be washed away, making it difficult for trees to reestablish themselves, as well as making the land unsuitable for agriculture. Today, loggers are encouraged to fell trees with more care, thinning the forest by selectively removing only some of the trees.

Mining

Over the centuries, people have been drawn to the Canadian and Russian taiga in search of gold and other precious metals. Many of the mines and smelters (metal extraction plants) have grown without adequate environmental controls. Mines create craters and heaps of unwanted dirt and rock. They are serviced by roads and temporary settlements that cut into the forest. Smelters produce pollution, which is spread around the taiga by the wind and rivers.

Miners pan and dig for gold in the Klondike Mountains of northwestern Canada during the gold rush at the beginning of the 20th century.

Fossil Fuels

In the 1960s, huge reserves of oil and natural gas were discovered in Siberia. This made Russia one of the world's largest fuel producers and created great wealth—but at the expense of the environment. In the taiga's harsh climate, the pipelines and drilling facilities are not easy to maintain, and leaks are common. A 2009 report highlighted the negative impact on wildlife of tar sands exploitation in the taiga forests of Alberta, Canada.

EAST ASIAN TAIGA

The East Asian taiga is home to some of the world's rarest animals, including Siberian tigers and snow leopards. Because of the region's wet summers and cool winters, the taiga extends farther south here than elsewhere in Asia.

Laptev Sea

New Siber Islands

! 1

4 Verkhoyansk

Verkhoyanskiy Mountains

Lena River

Yamma River

3 Yakutsk

RUSSIA

Dzhugdzhur Ran

Sakh Isla

Stanovoy Mountains

Heilongjiang

2

Amur River

Khabarovsk

5

Qiqihar

Harbin

Lake Khanka

Hokka

CHINA

Changbai Shan

Vladivostok

Sapporo

NORTH KOREA

Sea of Japan

P'yongyang

Honshu

Seoul

SOUTH KOREA

Yellow Sea

Osaka

Tokyo

JAPAN

Fact File

▲ Large-scale deforestation and acid rain have damaged much of Japan's taiga forest.

▲ Houses in Yakutsk are built on stilts to keep the buildings' heat from melting the permafrost beneath.

▲ The Siberian, or Amur, tiger (left) is the world's largest cat. In winter its red-striped fur becomes paler. About 500 of these tigers are left in the wild.

East Siberian Sea

Chukchi Peninsula

Kolyma River

River

● Magadan

Sea of Okhotsk

Kamchatka

⑧ ❗

● Petropavlovsk-Kamchatskiy

Bering Sea

Aleutian Islands

Kuril Islands

⑦

Pacific Ocean

| 0 | | 500 | miles |
| 0 | | 500 | kilometers |

NORTH AMERICA
SOUTH AMERICA
EUROPE
AFRICA
ASIA
AUSTRALIA
ANTARCTICA

1. Lena River
One of the longest rivers in the world, flowing 4,400 kilometers (2,734 miles) from its source in the mountains west of Lake Baikal to the Arctic. Parts of the river are polluted by fertilizers.

2. Heilongjiang
Although it is close to one of the most heavily industrialized regions of China, Heilongjiang province is still thickly forested and home to the nomadic Oroqen people. Bears and tigers are protected in the forests.

3. Yakutsk
A bitterly cold city for much of the year, this was a favored place to send Russians into exile. Today, diamond mines have made Yakutsk a prosperous city.

4. Verkhoyansk
Temperatures can fall to as low as −68°C (−90°F) in this small Siberian town, making it the coldest town in the world.

5. Sakhalin Island
This island was once a haven for wildlife. Today it is heavily industrialized and much of the forest has been removed. Pollution from industry and volcanoes is a problem for the islanders.

6. Honshu
The mountain forests of northern Honshu are home to Japanese macaques, the only monkeys to live in taiga.

7. Kuril Islands
The hundreds of desolate Kuril Islands hold great mineral resources. Russia and Japan are still arguing over who owns them. In recent years, the region has been shaken by earthquakes.

8. Kamchatka
This mountainous region contains more than 60 active volcanoes. Rare gyrfalcons are taken from the wild to be kept as hunting birds.

China's Forest Nomads

Until the last 30 years, the Oroqen of northern China (right) lived a nomadic, hunting lifestyle similar to that of traditional Siberian forest dwellers. They herded caribou, hunted deer, and lived in tents covered with birch bark in summer and deer skins in winter. Today they live a more settled lifestyle, with modern conveniences such as radio and television. However, many still wear traditional clothes, including a hat made from a deer head, complete with antlers. This is worn by men when they hunt deer. Oroqen women continue to make household items and canoes from birch bark.

THE FUTURE

Largely untamed, the taiga has escaped much of the impact of the modern world. However, tourism, industry, and climate change all threaten to alter the biome in ways that we are only just beginning to understand.

The world appears to be warming up. In 2007, the International Panel on Climate Change (IPCC) calculated that world temperatures could rise as much as 6.4 °C (11.5°F) by the end of the 21st century. This would have many effects across the globe; for example, sea levels could rise by about 0.6 meters (23 inches)—enough to flood many low-lying areas near the coast.

Scientists believe that the taiga is one of the biomes most likely to change in size as a result of global warming. If the world warms, the taiga might shift many miles to the north within the next few centuries. As this happens, the bands of taiga forest around the world could also shrink in size.

If the taiga biome does get smaller, this may have an added effect on global warming. As trees grow, they take in carbon dioxide from the air during photosynthesis and turn it into sugar and wood. The sugar is the trees' fuel, and when it is used up, it is released back into the air as carbon dioxide. However,

Climate Change

Scientists believe that the cause of global warming is the buildup of carbon dioxide and other gases in the atmosphere. Carbon dioxide is released when fossil fuels, such as gasoline, coal, and natural gas, are burned. Carbon dioxide is a greenhouse gas. It acts like glass in a greenhouse, trapping heat in the atmosphere and warming the planet's surface. Methane and water vapor are other greenhouse gases. Methane is released when dead material decays, from cattle, and from paddy fields, and water vapor is added to the air when things are burned.

the carbon in the wood stays locked up in the tree until it eventually dies and decays.

When a new forest grows, it takes in more carbon dioxide than it gives out. If a forest is cut down and burned or left to decay, it releases all its carbon into the atmosphere. If global warming causes the taiga and other forest biomes to shrink in size, the overall number of trees will be reduced. The carbon in the trees that die away as the biomes shrink will be released into the atmosphere, making global warming even worse.

Within the taiga, the distribution of forest trees will alter as global warming increases. Mixed forests—containing both deciduous and coniferous trees—will probably become more widespread and extend farther north, while the taiga as a whole gets smaller.

Sustainable Use

Sustainable use means harvesting natural products at the same rate that they can replace themselves. In sustainable taiga forests, only a few trees are felled at a time. These are replaced by natural growth without the forest getting smaller overall.

An oil pipeline cuts through a taiga forest in Alaska. The pipe is held above the ground so that the oil it contains does not warm the ground and damage the permafrost.

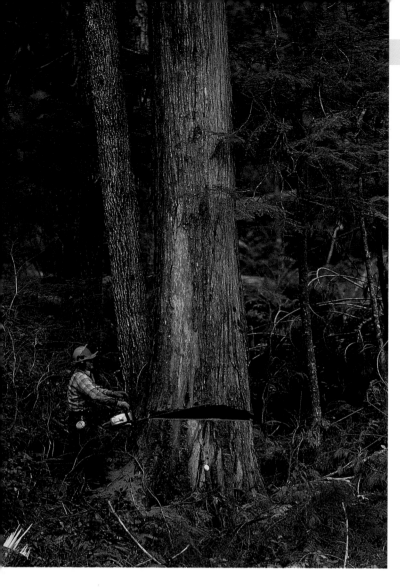

A lumberjack cuts through the trunk of a massive tree on Vancouver Island, Canada, as part of a sustainable selective-logging operation.

One of the best ways to conserve forest is to establish protected reserves in which the wood is harvested in sustainable ways. Instead of felling all the trees in an area—a practice known as clear-felling—lumberjacks are more selective in what trees they choose to remove. By leaving many trees in place and allowing younger trees to grow in the gaps, the soil is protected from erosion, and the forest floor keeps its cover of rare wildflowers, such as orchids. Consumers can also help protect forests by buying wooden and paper products that come only from sustainable forests.

Fire Hazard

Fire plays an important natural role in the ecology of forests, helping to maintain a rich diversity of habitats by creating clearings. However, with global warming, fires are becoming too destructive. Across the North American taiga, the area of forest that

 ## Saving the Planet

The Pechoro-Ilychskiy Reserve lies on the western slopes of the Ural Mountains in Russia. It was set up to protect areas of taiga, tundra, and alpine meadow. Its taiga regions include lowland pine forest, sphagnum bog, and foothills of dark taiga (fir and spruce).

Set up in 1930, the reserve was reduced to about 10 percent of its original size in the 1950s, but was enlarged again, in 1959, to about 60 percent of its original size. Between the 1950s and 1980s, some of the forests were cut down, and the moose and caribou, which had been protected, were hunted once again.

In 1984, the wildlife park was given international biosphere reserve status, providing greater protection. It remains an important place for animals and plants that are typical inhabitants of the European and Asian taiga. More than 500 species of flowering plants and 40 species of mammals, including brown bears, wolverines, pine martens, sable, red squirrels, chipmunks, and beavers, live in the park. It also harbors 200 species of birds and at least 17 types of fish.

Botanists and zoologists have studied the ups and downs of the resident populations over long periods. In the 1950s, the world's first moose farm was set up in the reserve. Scientific studies here make this among the world's best sources of information on moose behavior. The greatest threat to the reserve is not pollution but changes in government policy that could allow more development in the area.

Pollution Problems

When fossil fuels burn, they release chemicals that can cause acid rain. These chemicals—oxides of sulfur and nitrogen—can drift north from Europe, Asia, and the United States, producing acid rain in the taiga.

Acid rain damages trees directly (below right), scorching leaves, stripping them of their protective waxy coating. The leaves' pores are blocked by salts produced by the acids, so that trees can no longer photosynthesize efficiently. The acid can also release harmful metals locked in the soil, killing tree roots and affecting soil microbes. Overall, this weakens trees, making them more vulnerable to attacks by pests. Some trees are more susceptible to acid rain than others, so pollution can change the composition of forests.

Acid rain has another effect. It washes dissolved metals, such as aluminum, from the soil. These metals enter the taiga's lakes and rivers. The chemicals may kill all life and stop dead material from decomposing.

Pulp and paper mills and ore smelters can produce serious heavy-metal poisoning of rivers. Many rivers in the Siberian taiga are spectacularly polluted. For example, in the 1990s, cellulose-processing factories on the banks of the Amur River, which is near the border with China, discharged more than (38 billion liters) (10 billion gallons) of polluted waste into the river every year. Close to these outlets, all young fish are killed, including those of valuable commercial species.

burned each year in the 1990s was about double that of the 1940s. In Alaska and parts of Siberia this trend has continued.

Forest fires add carbon dioxide to the atmosphere, perhaps increasing the greenhouse effect and speeding up global warming. If there are more fires in the future, the tree composition of the forests will change. The trees that are good at resisting fire will become more common, as will plants that grow quickly from seed after fire has passed.

The Spread of Agriculture

Taiga country is not good for growing crops and raising livestock, such as cattle. Taiga people raise caribou inside the thick forests, since the deer can manage to exist by eating lichens, snow-buried berries, and mushrooms in the depths of winter. Cattle cannot survive the harsh winters, however, without fodder, such as hay, being given to them.

Despite the difficulties of raising crops in the harsh climate and thin soil of the taiga, growing cereals and vegetables has been a tradition among some taiga peoples in North America, Europe, and Asia. Wheat and rye for bread-making, and vegetables such as carrots and turnips, make a welcome addition to their diet of meat and fish. Nevertheless, forest clearance for these crops has had fairly little impact on the taiga as a whole. Of much greater impact is farming at the southern edge of the taiga.

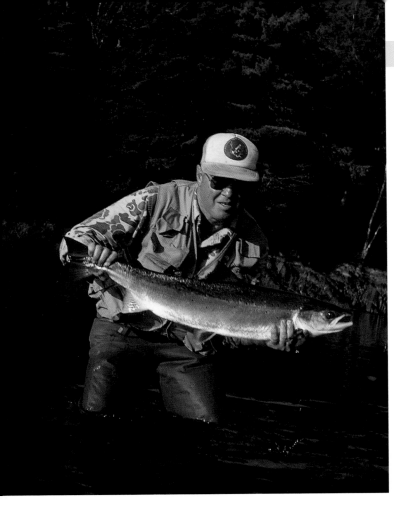

A salmon fisherman shows off his catch in a river in eastern Canada. Tourism and leisure are growing industries in taiga forests.

The southern limits of the taiga are being pushed farther north, as forests are cleared for growing crops and rearing cattle. In central Canada, for example, farmers combine cattle-rearing with growing cereal crops as cattle feed. The cattle graze on grasses sown under thin forests of deciduous taiga trees, such as quaking aspen and poplar. In British Columbia and Alberta, farmers grow cereals, oilseed rape for Canola vegetable oil, and plants to feed their cattle.

In the milder areas of southern Ontario and Quebec, clover, corn, and potatoes are the favored crops. As the human populations of North America and Russia rise, the desire to clear land along the southern edges of the taiga for use as farms grows ever stronger.

Canada's protected forests

There are two taiga reserves in Canada—Riding Mountain in Manitoba and Charlevoix in Quebec. The Charlevoix Reserve (below) contains fir, spruce, pine, and maple forest in the lowlands as well as mountain taiga. An important part of the reserve is the wetland drained by the St. Lawrence River and its tributaries.

Among the reserve's largest animals are the lynx, beaver, caribou, and blue snow goose. In the 1960s, caribou were reintroduced to the area. They had been cleared from the forests by hunting many decades before. The reserve is now a popular tourist destination, with nature trails, and with local scientists working to educate the public.

Riding Mountain National Park is an island of taiga forest surrounded by the prairies and wetlands of Manitoba. Riding Mountain is the highest point on the Manitoba Escarpment, which forms the centerpiece of the park.

Although it is a small park compared to North America's other reserves of taiga, Riding Mountain does not lack wildlife. In addition to wolves, black bears, and moose, the park is home to the largest herd of wood bison in the world. These animals are very rare and found only in the southern edges of North American taiga. However, the park animals are still at risk from hunters. Black bears and deer are lured out of the park with baits, where they are shot for sport. Bear hunting is legal in Canada, but shooting deer is not.

Managing the Taiga

Like many wilderness areas around the world, the taiga is being scoured for reserves of fossil fuels. The mountain rivers in the biome are also tapped for their energy. In Canada, for example, dams in the taiga provide 60 percent of the country's electricity. All this activity is changing the face of the taiga. Dams flood huge areas of forest, while trees cleared by oil workers in the far north of the taiga cannot grow back because the permafrost layer rises to the surface.

With or without global warming, the taiga will come under increasing pressure. As things stand, taiga forests may have been cut back by 50 percent or more, along with temperate and tropical forests, since people first began to fell trees. Scientists and foresters understand the simpler ecology of taiga forests better than the more fertile and complex temperate forests to the south.

This dam across a river in Canadian taiga converts the water's energy into electricity. The power is used by towns and cities far from the taiga.

This is a good starting point for the scientists, industrialists, and governments who work together to find ways to manage the taiga in a more sustainable way.

It is difficult, if not impossible, to put a value on the world's taiga forests. Their value lies not just in the wood they contain, or their ability to clean the air, stop flooding, or provide a living for millions of people. The forests, and the animals and plants within them, have a priceless beauty of their own.

 ## Saving the Planet

Some scientists suggest that planting more fast-growing taiga trees might slow or even stop global warming by absorbing extra carbon dioxide from the air. Unfortunately, the calculations do not add up. Much more forest would need to be planted than there is suitable space to do so. The best way to beat global warming is for governments to reduce the amount of fuels being burned, and to build flood defenses against rising sea levels. In the meantime, the taiga forests continue to flourish. Whatever the future holds, they are likely to last for many years to come, providing we keep a watchful eye on them.

GLOSSARY

alga (plural algae): A simple, plantlike organism that makes food from sunlight.

Algonquian: A family of Native American languages spoken by people in eastern Canada and the eastern United States.

Athabascan: A family of Native American languages spoken by people in western Canada.

arctic circle: An imaginary line drawn around the North Pole on which there is midnight sunlight for one day in midsummer.

atmosphere: The layer of air around Earth.

bacterium (plural bacteria): A single-celled microorganism; among the simplest forms of life.

biome: A major division of the living world, distinguished by its climate and wildlife. Tundra, desert, and temperate grasslands are examples of biomes.

bog: A type of wetland in which partly decayed plant matter builds up in soggy, acidic ground.

canopy: A layer formed at the top of a forest by branches and leaves. Some shrublands have a broken canopy formed by shrubs.

carbon dioxide: A gas released when fuel burns. Carbon dioxide is one of the main gases thought to cause global warming.

climate: The pattern of weather that happens in one place during an average year.

colonize: To establish a colony, or settlement, in a new region.

conifer: A type of plant that does not have true fruit like flowering plants but instead produces seeds protected inside a cone.

deciduous: A plant that sheds all its leaves every year.

desert: A place that receives less than 250 millimeters (10 inches) of rain a year.

dormant: So inactive as to appear lifeless. Plant seeds often stay dormant until their soil gets wet.

ecosystem: A collection of living animals and plants that function together with their environment.

equator: An imaginary line around Earth, midway between the North and South poles.

erosion: The gradual wearing away of land by the action of wind, rain, rivers, ice, or the sea.

evaporate: To turn into gas. When water evaporates, it becomes an invisible part of the air.

evergreen: A plant that keeps its leaves all year round.

fertile: Capable of sustaining plant growth.

fungus (plural fungi): A life-form, neither plant nor animal, that gets its food by digesting plant or animal material, living or dead.

geyser: A jet of hot water or steam produced by volcanic activity.

glacier: A river of ice that flows slowly off a mountain or ice sheet.

global warming: The gradual warming of Earth's climate, caused by pollution of the atmosphere.

hemisphere: One half of Earth. The northern hemisphere is the half to the north of the equator.

hibernation: A time of dormancy that some animals go through during winter.

hypha (plural hyphae): The thin fibers of a fungus, usually growing underground.

ice age: A period when Earth's climate was cooler and the polar ice caps expanded. The last ice age ended 10,000 years ago.

lichen: A partnership between algae and fungi.

mammal: A warm-blooded animal that feeds its young on milk.

migration: A long-distance journey by an animal to find food or a breeding site.

mycorrhiza (plural mycorrhizae): A fungus that is lives in partnership with a plant's roots.

nomad: A person who travels from place to place in search of food and water.

nutrient: Any chemical that nourishes plants or animals, helping them grow.

oxygen: A gas in the air. Animals and plants need to take in oxygen so that their cells can release energy from food.

peat: Partly decayed dead plant matter that builds up in bogs.

permafrost: Permanently frozen ground under the surface of some taiga.

photosynthesis: The chemical process that plants and algae use to make food from simple chemicals and the Sun's energy.

pollen: A dustlike powder produced by the male parts of flowers.

pollination: The transfer of pollen from the male part of a flower to the female part of the same flower or another flower, causing the flower to produce seeds.

prairie: A large area of grassland in central North America.

predator: An animal that catches and eats other animals.

protein: One of the major food groups. It is used for building and repairing plant and animal bodies.

rain forest: A lush forest that receives frequent heavy rainfall.

rain shadow: An area where rainfall is low because nearby mountains provide shelter from rain-bearing winds.

species: A particular type of organism. Cheetahs are a species, for instance, but birds are not, because there are lots of different bird species.

temperate: Having a moderate climate. Earth's temperate zone lies between the warm, tropical regions and the cold, polar regions.

temperate forest: A biome that mainly contains broad-leaved trees. Temperate forests grow the the south of most areas of taiga.

tropical: Within 2,575 kilometers (1,600 miles) of the equator.

tropical forest: Forest in Earth's tropical zone, such as tropical rain forest or monsoon forest.

tropical grassland: A tropical biome in which grass is the main form of plant life.

tundra: A biome of the far north, made up of treeless plains covered with small plants. Tundra begins at the northern edge of taiga forests.

water vapor: Water in gas form.

Further Research

Books
Cefrey, Holly. *Coniferous Forests.* New York: PowerKids Press, 2003.
Henry, J. David. *Canada's Boreal Forest.* Washington, D.C.: Smithsonian Institution Press, 2002.
London, Jack. *Call of the Wild.* Mineole, NY: Dover Publications, 1999.
(The famous adventure novel about a dog during the Klondike Gold Rush, which took place in the taiga forest of the Canada and Alaska around a hundred years ago.)
Nagle, Jeanne. *Coniferous Forests (Biomes of the World).* New York: Rosen, 2009.
Toupin, Laurie. *The Taiga: Life In The Boreal Forest.* New York: Franklin Watts, 2005.

Websites
The Boreal Forest Network: www.borealnet.org/main.html
(Information about North American taiga forests.)
Raincoast Conservation Society: www.raincoast.org
(Find out more about Canada's Great Bear Rain Forest and other areas of coastal taiga.)
Taiga Topics: www.mbgnet.net/sets/taiga/index.htm
(Useful site with facts about the taiga.)

INDEX

Page numbers in *italics* refer to picture captions.

acid rain 20, 31, 59
agriculture 59–60
Alaska 48, 50
Algonquians 48–49, 50
animals 23–24, 32–43, 54
Asia, East 54–55
Athabasca, Lake 8
Athabascans 48–49, *48*, 50

bears 32, *40*, 43, 55
beavers 36, 38
birches *27*, 29
birds 24, 36, 37–41, *37*
bison, wood 35, 36
bogs 17, *17*

Canada 8, 18
  reserves 60
canoes, birch-bark 53
capercaillies 36, *36*,
  37–38
carbon dioxide 57, 61
caribou 35, *40*
  people and *47*, 48, 59
China, forest nomads 55
clear-felling 52–53, *52*
climate 10–17, 31
climate change 8, 20, 57
  see also global warming
crossbills 41, *41*

dams 9, 19, 61, *61*
deforestation 9, 52, 54
  see also logging

European taiga 30–31
Evenki people 47
extinction 36

Finland 30
fires 21, 26, 58–59
firs *21*, 26, 27, *27*, 28

flowers 25
forests 6, 20–29
  clearing 7, 9, 52–53,
  52, 59–60, 61
  floor 23, 24–25
  and global warming 57
  North American 14
  open and closed 16–17
  sustainable 57–58, *58*
  see also trees
fruits 23–24, 50
fuels 53
fungi 22, *22*

ginseng 50
glaciers 20, 31
global warming 8, 9, 20,
  56–57, 59, 61
greenhouse effect 56–57,
  59

hares, snowshoe 35
hibernation 43
hunting, by man 36,
  51–52

ice ages 31, 46
insects 32–35, *32*

Japan, taiga 54

Khanty people *46*, 47

Lapland 30
larches 21, 26, 27, 29
lichens 23, *25*, 26–27
logging 36, 44, 52–53,
  52, 61
lynx 38

mammoths, woolly 31
marmots *42*, 43
medicine, from plants 50
mining 9, 31, 53, *53*
moose 32, 35, *40*, 49, 58

mosquitoes 32–34
mosses 8, 17, 25–26, 28

Native Americans
  47–49, 50
Nenet people 48
North America
  northeast 18–19
  northwest 6, 8–9
  people 47–49, 50
  taiga plants 27
nutcrackers 40–41

oil 9, 20, 30, 31, 45,
  53, *57*
owls 42–43

people 31, 46–53, 55
permafrost 16, 21
pines 26, 29
plants 8, 20–29
  for medicine 50
  see also mosses; trees
pollen grains 15–16
pollution 7, 20, 31, 45,
  49, 53, 55, 58, 59

rain forest 6, 8, *8*
redwoods 14, 27, *27*
reindeer *see* caribou
Rocky Mountains 12
Russia 30
  see also Siberia

Scandinavia 30
seeds 23–24

Siberia 7, 44–45
  climate 11
  fires 21
  people 47, *47*, 48, 49,
  51, 52
  permafrost 16
Siberian cranes *37*
snow *10*, 11, 21
soil 11, 13–16
spruces 26, 27, *27*, 28
stoats 35
sustainability 57, 58

taiga, open 16–17
threatened species
  animals 18, 36, 54, 55
  plants 20
tigers 36, 54, 55
totems *48*, 49
trees 8
  and acid rain 59
  conifer 6, 12, 13, 21,
  25, 27–29, 50
  deciduous 11, 13, 29, *29*
  and global warming 57
  world's largest 14
  see also forests

Ural Mountains 44, 58

water 10, *11*, 17 21
wolverines 36, 39, *40*
wolves *34*, 35–37, *40*
woodpeckers 38–40, *40*

Yakutsk 54, 55

Picture Credits

Key: l – left, r – right, m – middle, t – top, b – bottom.
Front Cover: NHPA. Ardea: Avon Dennis 41; John Cancalosi 51; Francois Gohier 26; Arthur Hayward 31 insert; Chris Knights 17; Stefan Mayers 42r; J. E. Swedberg 16, 60t; **Art Explosion:** 33t; **Bruce Coleman:** Natural Selection Inc. 11 insert, 12; **Corbis:** Yann Arthus-Bertrand 60b; Joel Bennett 48t; Bettmann 53b; Dean Conger 46; Richard A. Cooke 50; Wolfgang Kaehler 7m, 44, 45; Layne Kennedy 53t; Earl & Nazima Kowall 55; Joe McDonald 32; Neil Rabinowitz 48b; Paul A. Souders 49, 56; Karen Tweedy-Holmes 19; Kennan Ward 42l; **Digital Stock:** World Panoramas 7l, 30/31; **Image Bank:** J. H. Pete Carmichael 28; Steve Niedorf Photography 6r, 18; Paul Stover 22; Art Wolfe 6m, 8; istockphoto: 7r; **Jupiter:** Stockxpert 38; NHPA: B&C Alexander 47; Henry Ausloos 34; Laurie Campbell 21; Robert Erwin 25; Paal Hermansen 10, 24, 59; Karl Switak 14; T Kitchin & V Hurst 35, 39, 58; **Photolibrary:** Paul Taylor/OSF 36t; **PhotoDisc:** Geostock 61; Robert Glusic 4m; Bruce Heinemann 5l; Jack Hollingsworth 5m; PhotoLink 5r, 13, 23, 29, 52; Karl Weatherley 4r, 20; Jeremy Woodhouse 33; Public Domain: Larry Ward, Lower Elwha Fisheries Office 9; **Shutterstock:** Cindy Haggerty 54; Serhiy Kobyakov 25m; Savenkov 37.

The Brown Reference Group Ltd has made every attempt to contact the copyright holder. If anyone has any information please contact info@brownreference.com